Saints

To MB, my beautiful co-conspirator,
I love you with all my heart

Scot Bower

Saints

Illustrations by Linda Baker Smith

LION

A Lion Book
an imprint of
Lion Hudson plc
Wilkinson House, Jordan Hill Road,
Oxford OX2 8DR, England
www.lionhudson.com
ISBN 978 0 7459 5347 2 (UK)
ISBN 978 0 8254 7911 3 (US)

Distributed by:
UK: Marston Book Services, PO Box 269, Abingdon, Oxon, OX14 4YN
USA: Trafalgar Square Publishing, 814 N. Franklin Street, Chicago, IL 60610
USA Christian Market: Kregel Publications, PO Box 2607, Grand Rapids, MI 49501
First edition 2009
10 9 8 7 6 5 4 3 2 1 0
All rights reserved
Text Acknowledgments
pp. 15, 42, 50, 119: scripture quotations are from The Holy Bible, English Standard
Version, published by HarperCollins Publishers, copyright © 2001 Crossway Bibles,
a division of Good News Publishers. Used by permission. All rights reserved.
pp. 14, 18, 31, 47, 68, 81, 95, 107, 118, 120: scripture quotations are from the New
Revised Standard Version published by HarperCollins Publishers, copyright © 1989
by the Division of Christian Education of the National Council of the Churches of
Christ in the USA, and are used by permission. All rights reserved.
p. 28: scripture quotation taken from the Holy Bible, New Living Translation,
copyright © 1996. Used by permission of Tyndale House Publishers, Inc., Wheaton,
Illinois 60189. All rights reserved.
p. 65: scripture quotation from The New King James Version copyright © 1982, 1979
by Thomas Nelson, Inc.
p. 80: prayer taken from the Brendan Liturgy 'In Exploration of a Vision' in the
Northumbria Community's *Celtic Daily Prayer*.

A catalogue record for this book is available
from the British Library

Typeset in 10.5/13 Elegant Garamond BT
Printed and bound in China

Contents

Acknowledgments

The French have a saying, 'Knowledge is like jam; when you only have a little you spread it a long way.' That's how I felt as I sat down to write this book. Many great minds have reflected on the lives and legacies of the saints I am so fond of; for this I am incredibly grateful but also confess to feeling slightly intimidated. A list of some of the books and authors whose thoughts have in some way influenced this short book are found in the bibliography – please seek them out and give them the attention they deserve.

My personal thanks to all those who have helped and supported the writing of this book. My wife, Misty, and I are often staggered at the love and encouragement we receive from our many friends and wonderful family. We love you all so very much and we thank you from the bottom of our hearts.

Thanks especially to Humpty and Nana for allowing me to steal their beautiful daughter and grandchildren away, and for supporting us as our lives continue to be blown by the breath of God.

Finally thanks to Steph and all at Lion Hudson for giving me the opportunity to write this book.

Introduction
(My Story)

My cap is pulled down low, covering the dark circles which hide my eyes; it signals to those fellow passengers who might invade my space that I am not to be disturbed. This has been a long week and the twitch beneath my right eye pesters me to rest; to allow sleep – that which I have neglected for too long – to envelop me. But instead, I stir myself and with a sigh pull my notepad from my pocket and start to scribble. There have been too many friends made, stories told and sights seen for them to be forgotten. Somehow, I know that if I fail to record them now, even with my stubby pencil on paper, I will forget.

So I begin to remember; to retrace my steps of the last week.

My tiresome bus journeys to the Macedonian city of Ohrid and back were something of a self-imposed penance. I hadn't enough confidence in my aging VW camper van to risk the mountain roads, especially in winter, yet I couldn't justify the cost of a hire car. Sitting here gazing absent-mindedly through the window at the beautiful yet barren landscape, I'm smiling as I remember the outward journey from the capital, Skopje, which seems such a long time ago. The journey, though long, was full of amusing and alarming distractions; for instance a tiny elderly man would regularly stagger to the back of the bus and sit cross-legged in the aisle carefully setting up his gas burner to make sweet turkish coffee *for himself and our driver. If I'd thought the caffeine was going to get us there any sooner I'd have willingly got down on my knees and given the little old man a hand as he fumbled with matches amidst the nylon upholstery!*

Then, soon after pulling out from our rest stop at the mountain pass, an almighty explosion had me leaping from my seat like a frightened child, much to the amusement of my fellow passengers who couldn't have appeared less interested in the 'explosion' if they had tried. The loud noise that had sent me jumping into the aisle was followed by the quieter, comparatively more reassuring, flamp, flamp, flam, flam noise familiar to all who've been the unfortunate passenger in a car with a flat tyre. We pulled over and, just as I was internally promising to have more faith in my VW next time, and calculating how long it would take for a replacement vehicle to reach us, the driver and his caffeine-addicted friend got out to inspect the damage. After taking out the required amount of frustration on the poor wheel they folded a small piece of cardboard and stuffed it into the hole. I'm not sure I'd say this solution 'worked', but it did enable us to drive the rest of the way to our destination. Occasionally the card would have to be replaced and for the remainder of our journey we were passed by many an aging Yugo car and several horse-drawn carts, but eventually we trundled into Ohrid just six hours later than planned.

To say I wasn't in the best frame (or state) of mind to appreciate our destination would be an obvious understatement. I was all for grabbing a bite to eat and settling down for the evening. But as we walked laden with rucksacks down a cobbled street and turned a corner to face Lake Ohrid itself, I stopped. My mouth was open, yet no words came out. It sounds silly now but I was quite simply staggered into silence by the beauty of my surroundings. The sun was low in the sky and looked like it could have been resting on the tops of the mountains that encircled the perfectly calm waters which in turn reflected the bronze sunlight back at me. I stood on the edge of the shore beside small, brightly coloured fishing boats and watched silently for some time as the sun slowly sank behind the mountains, creating stunning silhouettes and shadows as it went. I was captivated.

In the days that followed, as I was shown around the ancient churches along the more ancient lakeside (Lake Ohrid is reputedly the third oldest lake in the world), my initial momentary captivation grew into a fascination for more than the natural beauty of my surroundings. I listened intently as I was expertly led from church to church and from monastery to monastery. We walked around excavated Byzantine church ruins the size of modern cathedrals (it is possible there were three such cathedrals in the space of several hundred square metres in the town of Ohrid. Two have so far been uncovered and ongoing archaeological digs hope to find a third). There were churches in caves on the beach and churches perched high up on cliffs overlooking the lake; some were hidden in the narrow streets and others sprawled with grandeur in the pedestrianized courtyards. Even to a postmodern missionary fool like me it was evident that this was a place steeped in Christian heritage.

Then, as we wandered back through the more modern pedestrian shopping streets, we came to a small enclave that was little more than a shrine; plenty of candles and some piped music were all that designated this patch of boulevard as any more special than the adjacent 'hamburgery'. Yet this was where it all began for this Balkan town. This was the site of the town's first church, long ago destroyed by an earthquake. There, casting a shadow over the cobbled floor as they gazed out across the still waters of the lake, were the bronze statues of Saints Cyril and Methodius, the patron saints of Europe. For the rest of the week I devoured stories of these saints and others from over a thousand years ago – stories of adventure and sacrifice; of miracles and of quiet prayer.

And as I sit here on this cold bus with its heady smell of diesel and strong coffee I scratch out some of the stories I've heard and begin to think of saints whose names I know, but whose stories I don't.

Those dreadful bus journeys that were sandwiched with a tremendous time with friends in Ohrid took place a little over two years ago. Since then I have travelled and read a lot about the saints. I must confess that I am no expert in saints and sainthood; I am a mere practioner – somebody who values and is fascinated by the stories and lives of those who have gone before me and attempts to use their example to inspire me and urge me on.

As missionaries in Eastern Europe, my wife Misty and I, as well as our adorable children Mimi (seven) and Evan (five), often find ourselves alone. But somehow, as we travel, uncovering the stories of a local saint helps to keep us sane, inspiring us us to keep going when times are tough – it is not for nothing that the Bible, in Hebrews 12:1, talks of crowds of witnesses that spur us on. These saints help to keep us humble when my foolish pride kicks in and I begin to think we are somehow special; that we are pioneering examples for the modern church. The saints remind us that great crowds of faithful men and women have gone before us and it is only thanks to their example that we are now able to walk along some well-worn paths. They are a gift that I am learning to treasure.

Misty and I are in the privileged position of being able to work with all kinds of churches and faith-based groups as we travel

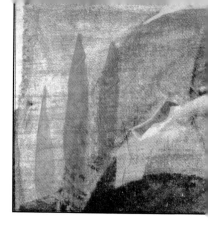

around Europe; from Orthodox
and Roman Catholic traditions as
well as a wide range of Protestant
streams. Working alongside such
a variety of people has helped to
increase my love and appreciation
for the complete Christian church.
Eastern churches, for instance,
have challenged me to consider more fully the mystical nature
of Christ and I'm often encouraged towards holiness and the
consideration of the sacrifice of Christ when I spend time with
Roman Catholic friends. Likewise my understanding of God as
Creator is grown when I come into contact with communities
with a Celtic flavour. Saints from these traditions also have their
own distinct attributes and yet all reflect the image of Jesus: in one
that reflection may be of his humilty; in another his authority;
in yet another his holiness. They all share a common devotion
to Christ, loving God, and serve those around them whether in
prayer or in action. They are splendidly diverse and yet in each it
is possible to see the qualities of Jesus Christ.

As a missionary, but more as a simple man who loves a good
story, I am drawn to mission-minded saints whose lives are full
of wandering narrative. And so it is mainly the tales of mission-
minded characters that you will read in the pages of this short
book, as these are stories and lives that captivate and inspire
me. However, I recognize that in so limiting the field we will
regrettably miss many figures from history whose lives may
not have blazed with such obvious adventure. These are lives
which should be allowed to inspire us nonetheless. My hope
is that by including here just a small selection of my personal

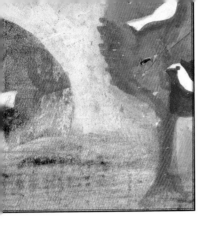

favourites from the first thirteen centuries AD, your appetite will be whetted sufficiently for you to continue in your own discovery of saints who become important to you. Whether particular saints are academics or apologists, contemplatives or hermits, or whether they are one of the many thousands of martyrs like Perpetua and Felicity whose names we know simply because of the lives they lost during the periods of Christian persecution, they each deserve our attention.

Before turning our thoughts to the particular saints, it is useful to say a word or two about the attempt to uncover the personalities of the saints and to separate fact from fiction.

Often saints are portrayed with a beautiful, golden halo that distinguishes them from the crowd. This 'setting apart' can be rather unhelpful in that it distances the 'holy' saints from the 'lowly' me. Perhaps the stories of their lives would become all the more remarkable if we brought these heroes and heroines closer to us. If we choose to recognize their humanity and identifiy with their frailty then we might better applaud their courage and determination, their discipline and their adventurous spirit. In the chapters that follow I will try to bring the lives of saints close enough to be able to take off the halos and look for the dirt under the fingernails and the laughter lines on their faces. So, as well as the historic significance of these heroes, each personality brings to us a fresh example in their character, be it the determination of Brigid or the humility of Cyril and Methodius, the servant heart of Martin or even the hospitality of Hild.

This book concerns itself chiefly with the saints that lived in the first 1,200 years after Christ, saints that were (generally) recognized and given the saintly status locally rather than through a later formal process of canonization. We journey from the Early Church Fathers (who provide the Christian church with a direct link back to the apostles of the New Testament), through to the close of the first millennium with the impending East-West schism of the church, finally ending with the new hope brought early in the second millennium by the saints of Assisi with their renewal of the monastic tradition.

It is often difficult, especially when dealing with notable figures who lived such a long time ago, to make the distinction between fact and fiction. Stories that are told and retold quickly become embellished, merged with others and eventually legends are sometimes born. At what point did the story of St George rescuing a village from monstrous wild beasts become the legend of St George slaying a fire-breathing dragon? Did Patrick actually banish snakes from Ireland? Did Brigid really continue to stretch her tiny cape over so many acres or did she just have a gift of persuasion? While some legends are difficult to believe when taken literally, the fact that they exist serves to some extent to validate the story itself. This book does not set out to prove a true historical record of the lives of the saints within, but nor is it a book of fairy tales. Somewhere in the middle of fact and fantasy are the stories of real lives which, through their retelling, became tales of adventure and heroism which have provided me with inspiration and challenge me to 'lead a life worthy of God' (1 Thessalonians 2:12).

CHAPTER 1

First Saints
Love and Devotion

Polycarp of Smyrna

> *Do your best to present yourself to God as one*
> *approved, a worker who has no need to be ashamed,*
> *rightly handling the word of truth.*
> 2 Timothy 2:15

The Early Church Fathers, or 'Apostolic Fathers' as they are sometimes known, hold a unique position in the history of the Christian church. They occupy that period which begins at the close of the book of Acts in the New Testament and ends at the beginning of the fourth century as the church moves from its position of persecuted minority to the accepted religion of an empire. These 'Fathers' were church leaders who carefully guided the followers of Jesus, guarding against heresy and false teaching from within and resisting the empire from without.

The accounts we read from these Church Fathers provide a valuable link to the life of Jesus and the teaching of the first disciples. They are the 'what happened next' at the end of the New Testament. Dionysius, for instance, who later became bishop of Athens, is reputed to have been in Egypt at the time of Christ's crucifixion. Later writings tell the story of how he witnessed the darkening of the sun for three hours and that he knew 'either God was suffering or the world was coming to an end'. Years later Dionysius was at Mars Hill in Athens and after hearing Paul's sermon on the 'unknown God' he believed and became a Christian (Acts 17:16–34).

Polycarp (AD 69–155) was the bishop of Smyrna (today the city of Izmir in Turkey), and is amongst the most venerated of the Early Church Fathers. Along with Ignatius of Antioch (today Antioch is the Turkish city of Antakaya close to the Syrian border to the south of Izmir) and Clement of Rome in the West, these bishops cared for the underground church in a difficult age and were martyred for doing so. Clement was drowned after being exiled to the Crimea, Ignatius was brought to Rome and thrown to the lions and Polycarp, as we shall see, was burned and stabbed. These, and countless other Christians, from the first 200 years after the crucifixion, steered the church through the heavy storms of fierce opposition and we owe them a huge debt of gratitude for doing so.

Much of what we know of these Apostolic Fathers comes from their own letters written to churches in their care. Clement wrote from the church in Rome to a church in Corinth urging peace and humility. Ignatius would appear to be the most prolific of writers and left seven letters to the churches as well as one to his co-worker Polycarp. Ignatius as the elder, more experienced bishop wrote Polycarp a letter that was full of practical wisdom as to how to perform the role of bishop and included an exhortation to the younger man to stand firm and strive for unity. 'Have a care for union, than which there is nothing better. Bear all men, as the Lord also bears thee. Suffer all men in love, as also thou doest,' he wrote. Polycarp himself wrote an epistle to the church in Philippi which also carries these themes of unity and grace.

There are many elements or passions that the early bishops and teachers held in common: they shared a dedication to the truth, a commitment to unity, a concern for the poor and they showed grace and forgiveness even to those who persecuted them. However, the life and story of Polycarp, which is full of simple humility and love for others, deserves special attention. Polycarp is also attractive because of what he was not: he was not a well-educated man, he was no scholar, his writing is direct and gives away his enthusiasm.

The love Polycarp showed for others shines out in a letter he wrote to the Philippian church, and it is also present in the story of his martyrdom. This love must have come, at least in part, from his teacher. The very same John who was the apostle, 'the disciple whom he [Jesus] loved' (John 19:26); the John who was one of the pillars of the church (Galatians 2:9); this John was also Polycarp's teacher. We don't know the exact time frame or extent of the relationship, but as we look at Polycarp's life it is clear that the teachings of John had a profound effect on him. Perhaps by taking a look at the later life of John the teacher we will better understand the life of Polycarp the student.

The writings of John in the Bible are soaked in love. The Gospel of John, as well as the letters attributed to him, are full of encouragement to 'love one another' (e.g. 1 John 4:7 and 2 John 1:5) and there is a wonderful story of John's later life, which expresses the love the apostle had for people and the faith he had in the grace of Jesus.

After his return from exile on the Greek island of Patmos, John continued to work as an apostle in the region, appointing bishops, establishing churches in the East and encouraging and overseeing the development of churches. After teaching at one such church he spotted a young man in the crowd, pointed him out to the bishop there and commended him to take personal care of this boy. The bishop promised to look after the boy and John departed for Ephesus.

True to his word the bishop looked after the youth, feeding, housing, teaching and eventually baptizing him. After baptism, the bishop, believing his work was done, allowed the young man to leave his care. But the youth fell in with a crowd who soon led him astray. The gang's exploits escalated and they fell deeper and deeper into trouble. Eventually, the young man who John had picked out in a crowd became the leader of a group of bandits living in the mountains above the town, beating, robbing and murdering those who were unfortunate enough to cross their path.

Some time later John visited the town again to settle a dispute. Once the meeting had finished he enquired about the charge which John 'and the Saviour' had left with the bishop. Realizing who John meant, the bishop told John the boy was dead, 'Dead to us, he is the captain of a group of bandits, the fiercest the cruelest and the bloodiest.' John was so maddened with grief at the loss of the young man that he ripped his clothes, pulled at his hair and with tears streaming down his face, he asked for a horse. At once he left the church and headed for the mountains.

The old man on the horse was soon caught by the bandits and brought to their captain. The captain, on recognizing the apostle, turned pale and ran from the camp. Weapons still in his hands, he jumped a fire pit and made for the forest. John, forgetting for a short while his age, chased after him shouting 'Why do you run my son? I'm an old man' and 'Son, pity me! Why do you run? I'm old and unarmed. Stop, stand and believe that Christ has sent me.' These words struck the bandit as forcefully as a well-thrown rock. He stopped running and stood staring at the ground. He then let

the weapons that marked his guilt drop from his hands and began to tremble and wept bitterly. All the time the old man walked steadily towards him and as he approached fixed the young man with his eyes and held his arms out in an offer of acceptance and forgiveness. The unlikely pair, an old holy man and the bandit captain, embraced and the volume of tears that spilled from the bandit's eyes was enough for some to call this a second baptism.

Yet still the bandit hid away his right hand. It was the hand which had caused so much death and pain and he hid it with shame behind his back. John, seeing this, knelt in the mud and tenderly brought the guilty hand out into view and kissed it. In doing so, he demonstrated the love of Jesus to the young bandit. The unlikely pair rode back to town and John then stayed some time to ensure that the man had been truly brought back to the church.

This story speaks of John's love and devotion to humanity as well as his belief in the restorative grace of God. It's an example to all of us who have a tendency to give up on people or fail to see the potential which God may see in others.

Some say that Polycarp was the bishop in the story. To me that seems unlikely, although not impossible. However, he would certainly have heard the story and as he knew John well, its example would have had a profound impression on the man. He certainly wouldn't have wanted to make the same mistake as the bishop in the story.

Polycarp wrote to the church in the eastern Macedonian (now Greek) town of Philippi, which lay across the Aegean Sea from Smyrna. The letter encouraged the church to persevere, to stand firm in their faith and in unity and grace: 'Stand fast, therefore, in these things, and follow the example of the Lord, being firm and unchangeable in the faith, loving the brotherhood, and being attached to one another, joined together in the truth, exhibiting the meekness of the Lord in your intercourse with one another, and despising no one.'

Polycarp continued in this theme on a practical and personal level encouraging the church to pursue a couple who had fallen away, in the same way that the young man in the story had, and 'not to count them as enemies' but to 'call them back as suffering and straying members'.

Towards the end of Polycarp's life he travelled to Rome to meet with his Roman counterpart. The journey from Smyrna to Rome took many months to complete and would have been pretty hazardous especially for an elderly man like Polycarp. (One only has to take a look at Paul's account of his journey in Acts 27 and 28 to understand the dangers that could be found on that long sea voyage.)

During his time in the city, Polycarp and the Roman bishop continued to disagree over the day on which Passover should be celebrated. Having failed to come to an agreement they resolved to take Communion allowing the bread and the wine to be used as a symbol of the unity they could and should celebrate together even against the backdrop of their differences and diversity. This was a fragile moment for the young movement and the commitment of its leaders to grace and unity is a shining example for the church today as it held the church at the time together.

As leader of a growing number of Christians with responsibility for churches in the wider area, Polycarp found his time much in demand. Because of this he developed a habit of withdrawing from the city at night, escaping to pray in the countryside. Sadly

it was here that Polycarp was found by those sent to bring him to trial.

As a Christian and bishop of the church in the East, Polycarp would have been under constant threat of arrest and the prospect of martyrdom was never far away. Ignatius, when considering the probability of dying for his faith, had encouraged Polycarp to remain 'firm as an anvil when it is smitten'. How these words must have come flooding back when Polycarp heard that at last the soldiers had come to take him. The old man calmly left the home of the friends with whom he was staying so as not to endanger them and went to wait for the arrest in a nearby house.

Then, when he was discovered as he knew he would be, he

invited his captors to stay a while and eat while he prayed. And pray he did. It is recorded in the chronicle of his martyrdom that Polycarp prayed for everyone he had ever met as well as for the church worldwide. Again Polycarp's attitude leaves an example for us all.

Polycarp was brought into the city stadium and urged to deny Christ and to call Caesar 'Lord'. 'Say "away with the atheists",' they told him, referring to the Christians. Polycarp slowly and carefully looked around him at the guards and the stadium crowd. He paused as if to consider carefully his next words. Then in an act of defiance pointing his hand back towards them and looking to heaven he growled, 'Away with the atheists! Eighty and six years have I served Him, and He never did me any injury: how then can I blaspheme my King and my Saviour?' The bloodthirsty crowd, incensed at this insult and blasphemy against their emperor, demanded his immediate execution. Finding that the lions had been taken away for the night, they quickly busied themselves collecting wood to make a fire on which Polycarp was to be burned alive.

As the guards roughly pushed the elderly bishop up onto the huge pile of wood, Polycarp asked for his hands not to be nailed to the post; he told them he would not try to escape but 'he who gives me strength will also enable me to remain at the post.'

Then Polycarp prayed a final prayer:

Lord, Almighty God, Father of your beloved and blessed Son Jesus Christ, through whom we have come to the knowledge of yourself. God of angels, of powers, of all creation, of all the race of saints who live in your sight, I bless you for judging me worthy of this

Clement of Rome

Clement, who died in AD 99, was one of the first bishops of Rome and his letter to the Corinthian church is the earliest and one of the most important pieces of literature following the New Testament writings. Clement addresses fractious disputes that have arisen yet again in the church of Corinth. Paul had written on much the same lines some years before. Clement's letter was written at the end of the first century and aside from being an important work in its own right, it points towards, and gives some evidence of, the martyrdom of the apostles Peter and Paul, who Clement says 'endured suffering' and 'bore witness'.

Clement was eventually exiled for his faith and taken as a slave to the Crimea. Here he worked alongside many other prisoner slaves in a quarry or a mine. Clement witnessed at first hand the suffering of his comrades who passed out in the heat and who were refused even a drink of water from their masters. In disgust, he strode out from the mine and went up a nearby hill. He took his wooden staff with him and once he had prayed, Clement struck the rock at his feet. At once a flow of water erupted from the ground and as a crowd gathered, Clement preached the gospel. Realizing that Clement was likely to cause them all kinds of trouble, the guards quickly decided to get rid of the bishop. They took him to the cliffs above the Black Sea, tied around his waist a heavy ship's anchor and threw him over the edge.

Centuries later St Cyril was on a mission in that region and discovered the bones of Clement, still with the anchor attached. He recovered the relics which during his visit to Rome some years later he presented as a gift to the pope. These important relics are housed today in the Basilica of St Clement in Rome.

*day, this hour, so that in the company of the witnesses
I may share the cup of Christ, your anointed one, and
so rise again to eternal life in soul and body, immortal
through the power of the Holy Spirit. May I be
received among the witnesses in your presence today
as a rich and pleasing sacrifice. God of truth, stranger
to falsehood, you have prepared this and revealed it to
me and now you have fulfilled your promise.*

*I praise you for all things, I bless you, I glorify you
through the eternal priest of heaven, Jesus Christ, your
beloved Son. Through him be glory to you, together
with him and the Holy Spirit, now and forever. Amen*

And with that the fire was lit. Those who witnessed the blaze told
how instead of Polycarp's body being consumed by the flames, he
appeared to glow like gold refined in a furnace and a sweet smell
of incense came from the fire.

Seeing that Polycarp was not touched by the fire, an order
was given to the executioner who came forward and stabbed
Polycarp with a spear. The account of his martyrdom tells how
the profusion of blood coming from his body was so great it put
out the flames!

In life Polycarp offered himself as an example to us of love,
humility, and unity. In death his final prayer is a challenge; how
do we cope with suffering; are we able to be thankful in every
circumstance as Polycarp did? In any case it does me good to
know that Polycarp is amongst those early saints who stand in
heaven and cheer me on.

When remembering the example of Polycarp, I find this prayer from the Roman Catholic Church heartening. It asks for courage in the face of suffering, just as Polycarp had the courage to endure the trials he faced. May we have a measure of that same courage to face the challenges of our own lives.

*God of all creation, you gave your bishop
Polycarp the privilege of being counted among the
saints who gave their lives in faithful witness to
the gospel.
May his prayers give us the courage to share with
him the cup of suffering and to rise to eternal
glory. We ask this through our Lord Jesus Christ,
your Son, who lives and reigns with you and the
Holy Spirit, one God, for ever and ever.*

CHAPTER *2*

Hermit Saints
Beloved Solitude

Antony of Egypt

> *As soon as Jesus heard the news, he left in a boat*
> *to a remote area to be alone. But the crowds*
> *heard where he was headed and followed on foot*
> *from many towns. Jesus saw the huge crowd as he*
> *stepped from the boat, and he had compassion on*
> *them and healed their sick.*
> Matthew 14:13, 14

Mother Teresa once said 'loneliness and the feeling of being unwanted is the most terrible poverty'. Loneliness has also been called a disease – it is one that is as prevalent in this age as the Black Death was in the Middle Ages. And yet we live in an age of noise and crowds. With today's technology we can talk to friends all over the world whenever we choose; emails keep us in contact as we travel and television shows a thousand faces each minute across a hundred channels. And yet there is no doubt that more and more people suffer from loneliness. We surround ourselves with electronic comforts and expect them to serve as a shortcut to relationship: television, radio and the Internet too all contribute to foster an illusion of belonging. Our subconscious screams at us to avoid the wasteland of 'loneliness' and so we surround ourselves with the busyness of crowds and constant noise. The result can often be that spending time alone, finding comfort in our own company or rest in our thoughts are skills and pleasures that have become devalued in our society and eventually lost to us.

But the dark loneliness of which Mother Teresa spoke becomes confused with the freedom that can be found in 'aloneness'. Loneliness has little to do with being alone – one can feel terribly alone in a crowded room, whereas spending time by ourselves, deliberately being alone, taking time and making space to unpick our thoughts and gain perspective, can be a most liberating experience.

The nineteenth-century poet Lord Byron explored the difference between 'aloneness' and 'loneliness' in his poem 'Solitude' from the epic *Childe Harold's Pilgrimage*. Here he deals first with the beauty and rest that can be found in aloneness, and then contrasts the brutal rush of loneliness:

> *To sit on rocks, to muse o'er flood and fell,*
> *To slowly trace the forest's shady scene,*
> *Where things that own not man's dominion dwell,*
> *And mortal foot hath ne'er or rarely been;*
> *To climb the trackless mountain all unseen,*
> *With the wild flock that never needs a fold;*

Saints

Alone o'er steeps and foaming falls to lean;
This is not solitude, 'tis but to hold
Converse with Nature's charms, and view her
  stores unrolled.
But midst the crowd, the hum, the shock of men,
To hear, to see, to feel and to possess,
And roam alone, the world's tired denizen,
With none who bless us, none whom we can bless;
Minions of splendour shrinking from distress!
None that, with kindred consciousness endued,
If we were not, would seem to smile the less
Of all the flattered, followed, sought and sued;
This is to be alone; this, this is solitude!

Antony of the Desert lived 1,700 years ago but his example shows how one can embrace aloneness and disentangle it from a fearful picture of loneliness. He was perhaps one of the first in the Christian tradition to give himself up to a life of contemplation away from the people he loved. His example has been followed by many through the generations and today this man who wanted nothing more than to practise a disciplined life of seclusion and simplicity is often cited as the father of monasticism (indeed the root meaning of monasticism comes from the Greek *monazein* – 'to live alone').

In life this barely literate man was so famed for his wisdom that philosophers from across the Roman empire came to converse with him. Even the Roman emperors of his day wrote to him for advice.

Antony was born in AD 251 in Alexandria, Egypt – one of the cornerstones of the Roman empire. We know his family were fairly well off and that they were Christian. Antony is said to have

shunned all other pursuits, academia and childhood play, to pursue godliness. As a young man his world was rocked by the death of both his parents. How they died is not known but their demise left Antony to care for his younger sister as well as for the household and estate on which he had been brought up.

Soon after his parents' death, Antony heard the words from Matthew 19:21, 'go, sell your possessions, and give the money to the poor'. This message struck him so powerfully that, after making provision for his sister, he sold the entire estate and distributed the proceeds amongst the needy. Shortly afterwards another message, this time from Matthew 6:34, reinforced it and changed the direction of his life forever, 'So do not worry about tomorrow, for tomorrow will bring worries of its own'. Antony pinned his life on these words of Jesus and with them ringing in his ears began his journey into the Egyptian desert.

Antony's contemporary and biographer Athanasius tells in *The Life of Antony* how Antony's hermit life, especially in the beginning, was a harsh battle with evil spirits who would attack him as he tried to sleep. Demons tried to tempt him back from the desert with images of the life he left behind. When that failed they tried to appeal to his senses with images of food or women. The attacks increased in ferocity but each time Antony was equal to the fight. One story ends with the pitiable 'spirit of fornication' weeping at Antony's feet; such had been the strength of Anthony's rebuke. On another occasion the hermit was beaten so badly by the spirits that his friend, who visited periodically to bring food, found Antony lying half dead on the ground. Athanasius describes how

Antony was taken to a village where he was laid out and funeral rites observed. The hermit woke during the night and pleaded with his friend to carry him back to his cave. Lying on his bed later that night, Antony called out to the demons, 'Look! Here I am, Antony, I do not run from your fights: even if you arrange more difficult ones, nothing will separate me from the love of Christ!'

This obstinate refusal to give in was characteristic of Antony's continual battle with the devil. On one occasion when he was attacked by demons who had taken on the appearance of wild animals Antony curtly told them, 'If you had any power, one of you would be enough for the fight!' Later he was to advise his followers simply to 'make the sign of the cross and depart without fear. Leave them [the demons] to mock themselves'.

Despite Antony's desire for a life of solitude and contemplation, of aloneness, he increasingly found others drawn to him: those who wished to follow his example: those who were in need of healing or deliverance from demonic spirits and those who travelled to engage in debate or seek advice.

On one occasion Antony had withdrawn and closed the door to his cell, refusing all visitors. An army officer knocked at the door begging Antony to heal his daughter. Athanasius records: 'Antony had not the slightest wish to open up but he looked down from above…' There is something rather amusing in this old man, who just wanted to be left alone, being besieged by visitors and yelling from what my brain naively pictures as an upstairs window. And Antony's advice to the officer is: 'Why do you ask me for help? Go and pray to God according to your faith and your daughter will be healed.' In other words, Antony was saying, 'Stop bothering me! Go and talk to God!' Another time, a sick man travelled from Palestine to Antony's mountain and asked Antony to pray for him to be healed. Obediently he prayed and told the man quite simply, 'Go and you will be healed.' The man refused and stayed where he was. Eventually Antony spells out his meaning to the sick man: 'You cannot be cured here. Go away! When you reach Egypt Christ will heal you.'

Time and time again men, women and children were taken to Antony in the hope that he would pray for them – and each time Antony encouraged faith and pointed only to Jesus and not to himself: 'No one should come to me, insignificant creature that I am, for the bestowal of cures is not a matter for human wretchedness, but for the mercy of Jesus Christ who always gives assistance to those who believe in him wherever they are.'

With these constant interruptions Antony withdrew deeper and deeper into the desert in order to find peace, but people still seemed to find him. Finally God promised to guide him to the inner desert so Antony travelled for three days through the blistering heat of the Sahara Desert and came across the only spring for many miles. And yet even there he was discovered.

And it was here, at this furthest point of withdrawal, that Antony finally became resigned to the fact that he would have to receive pilgrims. He even began to grow vegetables in a small garden in order to provide his guests with refreshment after a long journey. An amusing anecdote tells how Antony's first crops were eaten by animals. When he caught the culprits he gave them a telling off: 'Why do you harm me when I have done no harm to you? Go away and in the Lord's name don't come back!' Needless to say the pests left his garden alone after that.

Antony was sought out not only for healing but also for his wisdom. Athanasius records at least two such encounters. In the first the hermit is typically blunt in his response to two pagan philosophers who had travelled to engage him in debate. 'Why have you come to see a foolish old man?' he asked the travellers. 'Oh, but you are not foolish, but exceedingly wise,' they declared. Antony replied, 'If you have come to see a stupid man, your effort is wasted. If you have come to me because you think I am wise then you should imitate me and become a Christian. For it is right to imitate good things. If I had come to visit you I would imitate you, but as you have come to me in the belief that I am wise you should become Christians like me.' The philosophers went away 'amazed at his mental acuteness'!

The later visit from Greek philosophers is recorded by Athanasius in great detail. The visitors made demands of Antony to explain his faith and tried to impress and confound the old man with their superior education. The conversation is wonderfully played out, beginning, 'He [Antony] remained silent for a while, at first pitying their error.' Then Antony launched into a beautifully reasoned, systematic defence of the Christian faith and at the same time picked the religion of the Greeks to pieces. The monologue continues for nearly six pages with Antony, who had received little or no education, barely pausing for breath. At one point, Athanasius says, 'This argument caused the philosophers to look around at one another and mutter. Then Antony smiled and spoke once again…' A lovely summary of Antony's argument for Christianity comes a little over half way through the discourse; 'We Christians keep the mystery of our life stored up, not in worldly wisdom but in the power of faith which God has granted us through Christ.' At the end of the conversation, 'Antony stopped speaking and the philosophers, struck with wonder and amazement, departed from him after saying a respectful farewell, admitting to each other that their meeting had been of great benefit.'

Antony spent over eighty years in the desert and his reputation spread around the Roman empire. The emperor Constantine and his sons Constans and Constantius wrote to Antony often. We can only guess at the content of these letters; they may have been requests for advice and guidance in matters of empire or they could have been to do with personal salvation. Perhaps they were simply commending Antony's life. The hermit however was not impressed by this royal attention and it took the pleading of all his monastic brothers to coax the abbot into replying. 'What business do monks have with the letters of emperors?' he argued. When Antony did finally reply, the letter contained advice for the emperor to show compassion and justice and urged him not to neglect the poor, as well as reminding the emperor that imperial power was not as important as his personal salvation from Jesus Christ.

When judges of the law began to visit Antony bringing with them their prisoners in shackles, Antony wanted nothing more than to be left to his 'beloved solitude'. Yet, for the love of those who came before him, he never refused to give his counsel and advised the judges simply to put the fear of God above hatred and favour when passing sentence.

Eventually though, Antony would always be allowed to return to the inner mountain away from the hordes and, by this time, he would be somewhat protected from intrusion by the monks who had joined him. At one point, before retiring to his 'beloved solitude', he remarked that to take a monk from his solitude was like taking fish from water; if they stay too long they die.

Antony died in the year 356 at the age of 105 and he maintained a sense of humility even then. The practice at the time was that his body would have been venerated and many would come to witness the place where 'Abba Antony' was buried. Instead, Antony called his closest companions to him and had them swear he would be buried in the desert in secret and that they would tell no one of the location. Antony wanted nothing to detract from glorifying Jesus and was concerned that followers would seek the hermit and his grave rather than giving the thanks and praise to Jesus.

Today as we struggle to see the value of a life withdrawn from the world, the example of Antony teaches the tremendous value of times of seclusion and silence.

> *Jesus, just as you withdrew from the crowd to spend time with your father, help me too to find space in my daily life to withdraw. Be with me, Lord, as I find rest and wonder in my place of seclusion. And just as Anthony denied himself to serve you may I learn to deny myself and love you above all things.*
> *Amen.*

Wisdom of the Desert Fathers

The sayings of the Desert Fathers are jewels of wisdom from the brothers and abbots of the early Eastern monasteries. They offer profound insight not only into their lives – living as they did in quiet contemplation – but also into our busy twenty-first-century era. The sayings are not limited to one single author, but instead they show the wisdom of the Fathers who followed Antony into the desert.

The following deals with judgment and grace and is just one example from Abba Poemen.

A brother came to Abba Poemen one day. His heart had been troubled and he asked for permission to leave the monastery for he had heard stories which pointed out the sin of another brother.

'Are these stories true?' asked the Father.

'Yes,' replied the younger man. 'I trust the one who told me.'

'The one who told you is not to be trusted,' countered the Father, 'or he wouldn't have spoken ill of his brother.'

The old man then bent and picked up from the ground a slender length of straw. 'What is this?' he asked.

'Straw,' the young man answered.

The old man reached to the roof and grasped a timber. 'And what is this?'

'Why, that is the beam that holds up the roof,' answered the confused monk.

The old man looked into the eyes of the younger. 'You would do well to consider your own sin as the weight of the beam and that of your brothers to be like this single strand of straw.'

CHAPTER 3

Soldier Saints
Justice and Mission

Martin of Tours

> *… submit to one another out of reverence for Christ.*
> Ephesians 5:21

Martin of Tours was born in AD 316, just a few years after the Edict of Toleration was pronounced in AD 311. The edict was signed in Milan at a meeting of the two Roman emperors: Constantine who ruled in the West, and Licinius who ruled in the Eastern empire. This was not the end of the persecution that had marked the first 300 years of the Christian church, but it was an enormous step forward and brought Christian believers out into the open for the first time. Before this, conversations between Christians were hushed words accompanied by secret marks scratched in the sand; now members of the church could meet for discussion and worship together openly.

It was during this time that Martin lived and his example of a steadfast man in an age of flux is one that speaks clearly to our own changing world. There are many lessons that can be taken from his life. At times he stood up to human authority both declaring and demonstrating how the kingdom of God is at odds with the empires of his, and indeed, our age. At other times he would submit with humility to the will of others, relinquishing control of his life and simply trusting in Jesus.

Martin grew up in a small village in Pannonia, a region of what is now modern-day western Hungary, not far from the Austrian border. His father, an officer in the imperial army, made no secret of his dislike of this new religion and Martin, who so wanted to become a Christian that he was prepared to give up all he had in life, ran away seeking refuge with other Christians. Eventually Martin was hauled back to his family and the path towards his baptism and priesthood was blocked, first by his angry father and then by an unfortunate intervention from the emperor. The emperor had decreed that all sons of soldiers must become soldiers themselves, and as a son of an officer, Martin could not avoid the draft.

There are many stories which demonstrate Martin's concern for the poor and for those on the fringes of society. It was from his time as a solider that the most celebrated of these of these stories is drawn. It was a bitterly cold night and many in the city of Amiens had died that winter, succumbing to the freezing temperatures. Martin, then a cavalry soldier serving as part of the elite and rather smartly turned out household guard, rode through the gates of the city on horseback with several of his

comrades. The cavalryman sat far above the dirt of the street on his splendid charger yet did not fail to notice the old man who sat hunched on the street against the wall. The poor wretch shivered, hugging his begging bowl as if to gain some warmth from the empty plate. Sitting hungry and naked, the man was barely able to move, such was the cold that sapped the strength from his body. He looked up at the handsome rider and so much was said as their eyes met; the beggar pleaded as if for his life and the soldier,

recognizing the humanity in the naked old man, was moved into action. Martin took his white lambskin cloak – the garment of office for the household guard who were known as the *candidati* or 'men in white' – and hacked it in to two with his sword.

Leaving the beggar wrapped in the cloak, Martin spurred his horse on to catch up with the rest of his band. He could hear the laughter and see the scorn in their eyes as he approached but that night as he slept Martin saw a vision of Jesus wrapped in the same half cloak he had given the beggar. The words, 'Truly, I say to you, as you did it to one of the least of these my brothers, you did it to me,' (Matthew 25:40) drifted up to him.

It is not clear just how long Martin remained in military service; his contemporary biographer Sulpicious Severus is rather vague, but it is likely that he remained as a soldier for a full twenty-five-year term which was the requirement for all in military service at the time. It was only when he was forced to go into battle that Martin left the cavalry. He was conscience-stricken at the prospect of having to fight and he wrestled with how, as a follower of Christ, he could reconcile loving one's enemies with drawing sword in battle. He refused to fight and, accused of cowardice, was thrown into prison. Aghast at being called a coward he offered to lead the army into battle the next day, unarmed. Thankfully the enemy army sued for peace on the eve of battle and Martin was spared.

Throughout his military service Martin had continued his inward journey of Christian service, often being ridiculed by his fellow guards. Now he was finally free to pursue a life of quiet service as a monk. He had heard much of the Eastern monastic tradition and desired the life of quiet contemplation which he saw there. He had begun his journey to become bishop of Tours.

On leaving the army Martin sought out Hilary, the bishop of Poitiers, who at once offered him an appointment as deacon. Martin, humble as ever, refused but eventually agreed to join a minor order as an 'exorcist', a fourth-century porter and very much at the bottom of the religious pecking order. It was perhaps this obvious humility that years later was to play a significant role as his life once again took an unexpected turn.

Now serving as a monk Martin had at last found happiness and peace in the solitude of his position. Unfortunately this peace was not to last long. Soon after the death of his friend and mentor Hilary, Martin was approached to take up the position of bishop for neighbouring Tours. The poor monk was horrified by the idea, as we might expect from a man who had turned down deaconship to wait on tables, and who later also had to be cajoled by Hilary into accepting priesthood. He felt far from worthy of such a position. However life once again steered its own path for this saint. The people of Tours had set their hearts on having the humble monk as their bishop and hatched a plot to get their way. One citizen travelled to Martin and pleaded with him to come and pray for his sick wife. Martin naturally agreed and accompanied the man back to Tours. The closer he got to the town the more people lined the streets providing him with an escort all the way to the city. Shortly after this he was confirmed as bishop of Tours, despite opposition from several conservative bishops who regarded Martin as 'despicable: a person with such a scruffy appearance, dirty clothes and unkempt hair'.

Once again Martin submitted himself to a path he had not chosen and quickly immersed himself in the work. However, he changed very little in the way he conducted his life and lived in relative seclusion two miles outside of the town in a small wooden cell at a sheltered spot near the Loire River. This apparent isolation in no way diluted or distracted his love for the people he was charged with caring for. Severus writes: 'There was the same humility of heart, the same poverty of clothing. Full of humility and grace, he fulfilled the high office of bishop without abandoning his monastic commitment and virtue.' Whereas Antony of the Desert perhaps saw others as a hindrance and took himself further and further from the crowd, Martin was much more comfortable around people. Wandering among the villages and villagers he maintained a healthy balance between solitude and company.

Martin in fact cared for the poor, for the sick and for the forsaken in his society. He once heard how a wicked landowner and magistrate returned to Tours driving before him through the streets men in shackles. These men were criminals, or more likely, prisoners of war that the count intended to cruelly execute en masse and without trial the next day. Martin heard of this after nightfall and immediately made his way to the magistrate's castle where, having been unable to stir the occupants, he settled down to sleep outside the door. The magistrate was abruptly awoken by 'the blow of an angel' (one can only imagine the force and ferocity of a blow from an aggrieved angel and how it would be to be awoken in such a way!). The angel told him to get up. How dare he sleep while Martin was at his door! The drowsy count sent guards to look for the bishop but again and again they came back to tell him the holy man was not there. Eventually the count pushed the men aside and went to look for himself. After much searching he discovered Martin curled up at his door. Convinced by the Holy Spirit he blurted out, 'There is no need for you to speak: I know what you wish: I see what you require: depart as quickly as possible, lest the anger of heaven consume me on account of the injury done to you...' The captives were released and the morning's mass execution was cancelled.

Martin's words and presence carried a weight of authority far beyond the ordinary landowners. He was known to have been sought out by the Roman emperor Maximus on several occasions. These meetings give us an interesting insight into Martin's relationship with earthly authority. On the first occasion that the bishop accepted an invitation to dine with the emperor, an offering bowl of wine was brought out during the meal and passed to the emperor. Maximus, choosing to honour Martin, deferred to him and passed the small bowl to the bishop. Martin, having drunk, did not follow protocol and instead of passing the wine back to the emperor, rose and walked across to the priest who had accompanied him and offered the bowl to the little man of God. In Martin's world-view the kingdom of heaven had little to do with either one's position in society or the esteem of men.

Throughout his time in Tours, Martin continued to challenge the wider church, refusing to be ruled by 'the party line'. He was a constant thorn in the side of his superiors in the church as well as of the emperor. In a controversy of the time, he was careful to distinguish between heresy and heretic, and at one point appealed directly to the emperor for the lives of two bishops, Priscillian and his supporter Instantius, who were convicted of heresy and sentenced to death. He also insisted on the division between Church and State. How, he challenged, could the state convict on matters of church? (He did not argue that these Spanish bishops were not guilty but he was adamant that it was not the job of the empire to rule on their punishment.) Soon after this protracted affair, Martin, for the sake of church unity, took communion with his fellow bishops but it was the last time he would do so. Thereafter he refused to attend the synods or gatherings of bishops and concentrated on simply fulfilling his calling amongst the people of Tours and the surrounding area.

And it was in Tours in 397 that Martin died. He died as he had lived, caring for those around him, putting their needs before his own and submitting his life to the will of Jesus Christ. Sulpicious Severus describes the scene well:

Martin called his brethren to his death bed and told them he was dying. Great sorrow gripped his hearers, and there was only one cry in the midst of all their tears: 'Father, why are you deserting us? To whose care are you leaving us in our grief? The wolves in their savagery will fall on your flock! When you, our shepherd, are dead, who will save us from their teeth? Oh we know you are weary for Christ, but that reward of yours is sure and it will not grow less for the waiting. Oh, pity us whom you are leaving desolate.'

Martin was deeply moved by the tears which stirred the life-long sympathy in him that flowed from the heart of God's mercy. He too wept, we are told, then turned to God and, as his answer to their pleading, he made this prayer: 'Lord, if I am still needed by your people, I will not refuse the work. Your will be done.' Neither toil nor death could defeat him. Indifferent alike to life or death he would not refuse the one or fear the other.

And with this final act of his servant heart he passed on and leaves today the legacy of his life as an example in preferring others and submitting to the twists and turns our own lives take.

The life of St Martin of Tours is an example to us in many ways. His desire for justice, compassion for the poor, and the way he lovingly made disciples of so many young monks and priests are an inspiration. He lived in a time of change yet was consistent and steadfast to the point of stubbornness. And it is this ability to live a consistent life, to accept all that life brought, laying aside his own desire for quietness to serve in whatever way was asked of him, that maybe we can best draw inspiration from. Again and again Martin laid aside his own dreams, echoing Jesus' own words from Luke 22:42, 'not my will, but yours be done'.

Martin's attitude is well summed up in the words of the Methodist covenant prayer written by John Wesley and used by Methodists all over the world as they renew their commitment to God each year:

I am no longer my own but yours.
Put me to what you will,
rank me with whom you will
put me to doing,
put me to suffering;
let me be employed for you,
or laid aside for you,
exalted for you,
or brought low for you;
let me be full,
let me be empty,
let me have all things,
let me have nothing:
I freely and wholeheartedly yield all things
to your pleasure and disposal.
And now, glorious and blessed God,
Father, Son and Holy Spirit,
you are mine and I am yours.

Boris and Gleb

The brothers Boris and Gleb were the favoured sons of the Kievan king, Vladimir the Great, and heirs to his throne. At some point during their father's lifetime they converted to Christianity, and this had a profound effect on how they lived and ended their lives.

After the death of the king c. 1015–19, his third son, Sviatopolk, seized the throne. Sviatopolk then hatched a plan to kill off his brothers in order to secure his position as king and successor. Interestingly Boris and Gleb both refused to fight him and instead prayed for their brother. In the end, Boris was set upon by a band of armed men after evening prayer and as he was stabbed to death, he uttered a few words of prayer, 'Hold it not against him [Sviatopolk] as a sin, O Lord!' Gleb too refused to take arms against those who were coming to kill him and had his throat cut with a kitchen knife by his own cook.

Both brothers, although heirs to the throne, chose to embrace martyrdom rather than to strike an enemy. It is somewhat ironic therefore to see these pacifist brothers represented in icons in the Eastern church as soldiers sitting high on their horses with spears in their hands. But such are the twists of history that heroes or anti-heroes have greater appeal as soldiers on horseback rather than as priests on their knees.

CHAPTER 4

Latin Saints
Stability and Obedience

Benedict of Nursia

> *Put on then, as God's chosen ones, holy and beloved, compassion, kindness, humility, meekness, and patience, bearing with one another and, if one has a complaint against another, forgiving each other; as the Lord has forgiven you, so you also must forgive. And above all these put on love, which binds everything together in perfect harmony.*
> **Colossians 3:12–14**

'Listen O my son…' This is how Benedict, the man who transformed the Western monastic movement, begins his 'rule'. And from these words the rest of his teaching flows. The command to stop and listen underpins everything that is taught and understood through Benedictine monasticism.

Much of the rule that was to later bring about the monasteries of the Benedictine or 'Black monks' (so-called because of the black habits the Benedictine brothers wore), with their mighty cathedrals and cloisters of England and mainland Europe, is summed up in that opening sentence: 'Listen O my son to the precepts of they master, and incline the ear of they heart.' By listening both to God and to those around us, we are able to prefer others; by choosing to listen and not to speak we make a conscious decision to put the other first. We learn to build each other up and through listening become obedient and teachable. Visitors to one Benedictine community in Ireland are asked to observe the ethos of the monastery and, while there is no vow of silence, they are asked to consider their words carefully. As words are very powerful – in the Bible, the book of James urges us to keep careful control of our tongue and reminds us of the power this small muscle can wield – visitors are encouraged to adjust their default attitude and response from one of speaking, to one of listening.

Benedict's rule was based on, and adapted from, 'The rule of the Master' and was written as an instruction manual for individual abbots of monasteries to explain the order of life that was followed by Benedict and the monastery at Monte Cassino in Italy, as well as those he had established elsewhere in the region. Although there were many other rules at the time, Benedict's is the rule which has remained highly influential and largely unchanged for 1,500 years.

In England the influence of Benedictine monasteries on society was extensive, especially in the later Middle Ages. At the time of the Norman Conquest, in the year 1066, there were fifty such monasteries in England and Wales. By the year 1200 this number had grown to 300, and by the time of the Protestant Reformation in the early 1500s it is said that a monastery of some description (for by then several streams of monasticism that had emerged out of the Benedictine model) was to be found within a day's walk of most homes. However, after Henry VIII was made supreme head of the English church in 1536, he ordered the dissolution of the monasteries, and almost all Benedictine monasteries in England were destroyed. The monks were scattered, the abbots executed and buildings, some of which had been magnificent cathedrals, were left in ruins or passed to the English church. Nevertheless, the Benedictine influence was not over.

However, a valuable nugget of Benedictine life remained and was transferred to the English church through the Archbishop of Canterbury, Thomas Cranmer. Cranmer took the liturgy and structure of Benedictine prayer and condensed them into the *Book of Common Prayer*. This little book became – and remained – the backbone of the English church services until recent times.

Benedict was born in 480 in a small town at the foot of the magnificent Umbrian mountains of central Italy, into a relatively upper-class family. While the natural countryside of Benedict's birthplace was beautiful, the political and religious landscape was in turmoil, for the Roman empire had been crumbling for some time. The historian Hans Lietzmann remarks that the empire in AD 268 'was bleeding from a thousand wounds' and notes that the lasting memorials to the emperor of the time, Aurelian, were the walls of Rome which still stand in part today, 'The walls offered an impressive sign of the times. Previously the walls of Rome were found on the Rhine and the Danube, and in the fortresses built in the Syrian wilderness.'

The erection of defensive walls around the city was certainly a visible demonstration of the vulnerable state of the empire. Rome finally fell at the hands of the marauding Visigoths from the East in 410. This was the first time in 800 years that the mighty city and and heart of the empire had fallen and now the Italian states had been drawn into the general mêlée of the battle for Europe. Rome was no longer the untouchable seat of a great empire it had been just 100 years earlier. The Christian church too was experiencing significant trouble, most notably in the age-old differences in practice as much as theology, between the Eastern and Western church. It hadn't yet reached the point of the schism that still separates the two churches today, but division was becoming more and more evident as the different centres of ecclesiastical power battled for supremacy. And so it was into this fractious time that Benedict was born.

After a safe and secluded childhood in the provinces, the young Benedict left Umbria and travelled to the metropolis in order to further his education and study literature. However, it wasn't long before Rome became too much for him. He despaired at seeing so many of his fellow students fall headlong into the vices of the city. Pope Gregory I, who wrote a short biography of Benedict fifty years after the monk's death, tells how Benedict had pulled himself back from the 'brink of a bottomless abyss'. Faced with temptation, Benedict chose to flee the city taking his nurse with him as his only companion. Together they journeyed into the mountains about forty miles from Rome.

Benedict, after a short time living in a small mountain village, soon took the decision to emulate the Eastern desert monks and withdrew from society completely. He walked into the mountains finding solitude in a small cave above a river. But this withdrawal did not happen before he had performed his first miracle, also recorded by Gregory. The act was simple and were it not for the later teaching of Benedict it could be overlooked. Benedict found his nurse in tears crying because she had broken a cooking sieve borrowed from a neighbour. Young Benedict, seeing his nurse in tears, took the broken sieve and began to pray. On his knees, he too was crying and when he finished his prayers he looked to his side and found the sieve perfectly restored. This simple unglamorous story demonstrates the importance that Benedict places on the sanctity of service. The rule he later wrote emphasizes that monastic life is to be balanced and no one activity is more pleasing to God than any other.

All tools too were to be valued just as if they were used at the altar. In 2 Kings 6, a member of Elisha's party loses the axe-head as he cuts down trees. This story is echoed when Gregory later tells of a young and enthusiastic monk in Benedict's monastery whose task that day was to clear away some nasty thorns and shrubs which were growing beside the lake. The man was swinging his scythe vigorously, cutting through the thorns when a particularly athletic swing caused the iron blade to come away from the wooden handle. The monk watched open-mouthed as the cutting end of his valuable tool sailed up and over the rest of the shrubs, landing well out of reach in the middle of the lake. Shocked and ashamed he reported the loss, and the news was soon heard by Benedict. The abbot quickly rose and marched towards the lake, grabbing the handle from the sorry young monk as he stormed past. Kneeling at the water's edge the abbot plunged his arm with the wooden shaft in hand into the cool, clear water. After a moment the abbot rose and, as he withdrew his hand, the brothers saw the blade was now reattached to the handle. The abbot handed the scythe back to the astonished junior and bade him to carry on the work but to perhaps do so a little more carefully and a little less enthusiastically.

In today's culture we assign different values to different tasks and yet Benedict taught that all activity should be seen as holy. All spiritual, physical and mental 'work' – whether it was prayer, the chopping up of wood or the illumination of manuscripts – all were equally important and should be held together in balance, each being undertaken as worship to the glory of God. Benedict might teach today that whether the task in front of us is to cook a

meal for our family or to work a day at the office – whatever it may be – we should see it as a valid and important act of worship.

Having lived in his cave for some years Benedict's fame in the region grew, and he began to attract the attention of a local monastery whose abbot had recently passed away. The monks pestered Benedict to take over as head of their monastery but he refused. He told them his ways would not suit them, but again and again they came back, begging him to reconsider. There was considerable gravity attached to the role of an abbot which Benedict took particularly seriously. The abbot was seen as representing Christ amongst the brothers. He was to be obeyed at all times and would eventually stand in front of God to give an account not only for his own life and teaching, but that of all those monks whom he accepted into his care.

Eventually, and very reluctantly, Benedict consented to their pleas. However it didn't take long for the monks to realize that while Benedict's strict lifestyle had been wonderfully impressive to observe from a distance, to put themselves under his authority was rather more of a challenge than they had anticipated. Things that had previously been allowed in the monastery were now denied to them. Benedict was unrelenting in his strict fathering of the community and after some infighting the desperate monks hatched a plot to do away with their 'tyrant' ruler and attempted to poison the new abbot. From Gregory's account it would seem that poisoning was something Benedict endured fairly regularly in his later life from those who took exception to him and his teaching. On this, the first occasion, the monks poisoned his wine. Then as Benedict lifted the goblet to bless the wine and made the sign of the cross the cup exploded as if hit by a stone and showered the assembled monks. The abbot got to his feet quite

calmly, brushed himself down, and gazed with pity and incredulous sadness at the junior monks. 'May God have mercy on you my brothers; why did you want to do this to me? Did I not tell you in the beginning that my ways and yours were not compatible? Go and find yourselves another abbot because after this you certainly can't have me,' he said.

Washing his hands of the unteachable monks and the monastery that was incompatible with his beliefs and lifestyle, Benedict returned to his cave and the welcome seclusion it afforded him. From this cave he began to gather those who could accept his teaching and established twelve small monasteries in and around the valley, each housing twelve monks – perhaps modelling Jesus' example of taking twelve disciples. These small monasteries, typical of the early Middle Ages and rarely bigger than the average household, were in sharp contrast to the huge abbeys of the later Middle Ages and also to today's value system where quantity is so often esteemed over quality.

As Benedict's influence and appeal grew, so too did the number and size of his monasteries and, while they were largely autonomous, Benedict remained in a position of authority over each of them. The following tale reveals much about the nature of the man and his rule which revolved around authority and obedience, that is, the authority of the abbot and the obedience of the monk both to Christ and to the abbot in charge of their monastery.

Prayer and the regular prayer times or offices were of huge importance to a monastery and Benedict wrote in great detail as to how and when these were to be conducted. Attendance was mandatory unless a monk was away from the monastery, in which case he was to perform the prayers alone but at the same time as his brothers back at the abbey. It was also necessary to be punctual. For those whose day's work had taken them some distance from the chapel, Benedict wrote that the prayer time should begin with the recitation of the 'Gloria', which should be prayed slowly in case there were those who may be late arriving. Only if a monk arrived after the completion of the 'Gloria' would they be punished.

Benedict heard from one of his abbots that one young monk easily got distracted and was unable to remain standing during prayer times, frequently getting up and wandering out from the chapel. Benedict therefore called on the monastery in question and witnessed the young man wander outside during prayer. Benedict said nothing at the time but prayed silently for his wayward brother. Two days later when the brothers emerged again from evening prayer, Benedict saw the young monk already outside leaning against a wall. The abbot marched towards the distracted brother and without pausing, struck the monk hard with his wooden staff. From that day onwards the monk joined with each prayer time without a problem!

Benedictine monks today continue to take a vow of obedience to Christ as well as to the abbot of their monastery, just as Benedict had laid out so many years ago. The obedience demanded of these monks is an 'obedience without delay', following the example of Jesus' disciples. Monks were – and are – to respond promptly to any instruction, and immediately and without question to the command of an abbot, even if they feel they have been given an impossible task. One of Benedict's miracle stories reported by Gregory, of which there are many, records how a monk who was sent to draw water from the river lost his footing, fell into the fast-flowing water and, being carried away by the current, began to drown. Benedict, who throughout Gregory's writings is shown to have demonstrated tremendous foresight or prophetic gifting, sensed immediately what had happened and ordered another monk to go quickly to the river. This monk, without pausing to question his abbot, ran from the monastery building and down to the river. He continued at pace walking, or rather running, on water until he reached the spot where he could see the younger monk thrashing away beneath the surface. He quickly grabbed the monk by his hair and hauled him to the surface then carried him back to land. It was not until he reached the shore that he understood quite what he had done; he would never have dared walk onto the water had he realized what he was doing. Later a conversation developed between this Peter-like monk (see Matthew 14:29) and the abbot. The monk insisted that the miracle was due to the order of the abbot, whereas Benedict was equally determined to attribute it to the monk's unquestioning and prompt obedience rather than the order itself. The soggy boy monk was called to give his account and settle the argument and told how as he was pulled from the water he could see the sheepskin of the abbot above him and saw Benedict's face as he was carried to the river bank.

After the call to obedience, central to the vow of a Benedictine monk are the values of stability and what is described by the Latin phrase *conversatio morum*.

Stability reflects the need to commit to place and people, or, as the apostle Paul put it, 'to stand firm'. When times become tough, or even when life seems dull, and something, someone or somewhere else catches the eye, to remain as and where we are is often the hardest choice to make.

Towards the beginning of his rule Benedict described the different types of monks. He regarded cenobites, or those who lived in community under the rule of the abbot, as the most steadfast class of monks, and his rule concentrates on helping them live out their lives in community. After praising cenobites Benedict mentioned another type of monk, the 'gyrovagues' – those who were unable to settle and instead spent their lives wandering from monastery to monastery, without the rule of the abbot or the fellowship and mutual accountability of brothers. Benedict declared these gyrovagues as abandoned to their own pleasure and refused to say any more than 'of their miserable way of life it is better to be silent than to speak'. These wandering monks would be thoroughly unable to take a vow of stability and so missed out on the difficult lessons that long term commitment can teach.

The second part of the Benedictine vow may seem to contradict the commitment to stability. *Conversatio morum* is a difficult Latin phrase to translate. The essence of it is a commitment to daily conversion and therefore constant change. A vow of *conversatio morum* is a promise to keep moving and accept change, but is to be understood in balance with that of stability. On one hand it is to stand firm against the flow of the world and the desires of the heart and on the other to accept the challenge to be continually

Gregory the Great

Pope Gregory the Great (540–604) saw great power in the teaching of Benedict. And it was largely thanks to his biography of the abbot himself that the Benedictine model of monasticism spread so quickly across Europe. With its highly organized structure and the level of authority that was invested in the abbot, the Benedictines became a useful tool in the Roman evangelization of Europe and especially of England.

Gregory had seen two fair-haired Anglo-Saxon boys being sold as slaves in Rome and had been told that these 'Angles' – or 'angels' – were from England. Then, some years later, he received a letter from the Celtic abbot Columbanus who was at that time based in Burgundy (see Chapter 5). Columbanus was writing to argue about the age-old issue of ecclesiastical dates. The Celtic Church was continuing to follow the Eastern calendar rather than that used by the Latin church, but perhaps the letter put the pope in mind of the angels he had seen and the desire to convert the English was stirred in him.

Gregory chose the abbot of his own small monastery of St Andrew at Celian Hill in Rome to act as his representative and soon Augustine set out for England. Augustine began his mission in the south of the country by converting the Kentish king Ethelbert and many of his subjects. He then established himself as archbishop of Canterbury, using that city as the headquarters of the church in England. He quickly planned for other bishops to be installed as he carried out the plan masterminded by Gregory to evangelize England.

transformed by the renewing of the mind to be more like Jesus each day.

Benedict died in 550 shortly after his twin sister Scolastica who had followed him into the monastic life and was herself abbess of a nearby convent. Both the 'life' and 'rule' of Benedict are full of encouragement which though written for monks over 1,500 years ago are in many ways useful for life today. To achieve the balance that Benedict established, listening rather than speaking and submitting our will to those we live with would make life for many so much better.

Towards the end of the rule is a wonderful summary of how life should be lived, sacrificially, but with friends who support and encourage one another:

Let them bear patiently with each other's infirmities, whether of body or of mind. Let them contend with one another in the virtue of obedience. Let no one follow what he thinks profitable to himself, but rather that which is profitable to another. Let them practise brotherly charity with love. Let them fear God and love their abbot with sincere and humble affection and let them prefer nothing whatsoever to Christ, and may He lead us all together to life everlasting. Amen.

CHAPTER 5

Wandering Saints
Pilgrimage and
Adventure

Brendan the Navigator

> *Then Jesus said to them, 'Follow Me, and I will make*
> *you become fishers of men.' They immediately left*
> *their nets and followed him.*
> Mark 1:17, 18

The Celtic Church had a term for those who abandoned themselves geographically to God. These were the 'white martyrs'. They gave up their homeland, their rights to belong and their place of belonging, to go where the Spirit of God blew them. Life for these saints was seen as one long pilgrimage. Increasingly during the Middle Ages this meant that the Celtic stream of Christianity spread from Britain across the English Channel and into Europe.

Pilgrim ways are still marked today in Cornwall from the north to the south coast where saints from Ireland and the north of modern-day Scotland landed. They crossed the country on foot to avoid the lengthy and dangerous sea journey around Land's End before sailing again from south coast ports to northern Brittany.

In 590, and at the age of forty-seven, Columbanus left Ireland, along with twelve men chosen from the famous monastery of Comgall at Bangor, and set out for Gaul as a 'voluntary exile for Christ'. He established an abbey in what is now the east of France and there he and his disciples lived and worked amongst the Frankish people. Their coexistence with the local Roman church was not easy, and they did not ingratiate themselves well with the ruling royal family. Eventually these quarrels escalated and after the abbot refused to baptize the illegitimate son of the local king, Theuderic II ordered that Columbanus and his monks be deported back to Ireland. Columbanus clearly loved his native Ireland and a part of him may have been relieved at the news he was to be sent home. But he had accepted God's call, he had already given up his right to a homeland, he was a wanderer, a *peregrinato*. When he had set out from the shores of Ireland he knew he would not return.

Columbanus and his Irish monks were force-marched the 500 miles to Nantes on the Atlantic coast where a ship was waiting. They prayed and sang as they trudged through the French countryside and continued to trust God in the midst of their sorrow, doubt and desperate hunger. It was only the kindness of the villagers they passed en route that prevented the monks from starving to death on the journey. When they reached the port they were manhandled aboard the sailboat. Then, almost as soon as the voyage had begun, it ended. Barely had they left the harbour

when the ship ran aground on a hidden sandbank. The monks took their chance to escape. Perhaps the captain decided to rid the boat of them or perhaps the monks in their simple habits broke out and jumped overboard having seen the guards heading out of town. We are left with the picture of a band of Celtic monks standing dripping wet on the shore side. Columbanus journeyed back across Gaul and headed for what is today the Swiss German border, establishing a monastery on Lake Constance. He never returned to Ireland but finished his days in northern Italy at the monastery in Bobbio, another of his plantings.

Columbanus is just one example of the wandering, pioneering spirit that characterized the Celtic way. Where the Roman Church established a vow of stability, a commitment to place, the Celtic Church encouraged movement expressing life as a pilgrimage.

This spirit of pilgrimage is wonderfully expressed in the life and legendary travels of Brendan (486–575). There is very little historical evidence about him, but the tales surrounding Brendan place him as a contemporary of the bishop Columba (521–97), who travelled from Ireland to establish the monastery on Iona. It is possible that Brendan also met St Brigid. He was said to have established many abbeys across Ireland, Scotland, Wales and also in Brittany.

In many ways the epic travels of Brendan echo the journey of the biblical figure Abram (later renamed as Abraham by God) as he set out from Haran. 'The Lord said to Abram, "Go from your country and your kindred and your father's house to the land that I will show you."… So Abram went, as the Lord had told him' (Genesis 12:1, 4a). Brendan too left his home with no promise of return and went in search of the legendary 'promised land of the saints'.

The legend of Brendan's journey as recorded in the *Navigatio Sancti Brendani Abbatis* (*Voyage of Saint Brendan the Abbot*) – the earliest manuscripts of which date from the tenth century – was widely read during the Middle Ages and subsequent accounts of his travels were translated into languages as diverse as Icelandic and Catalan. Clearly these stories had a huge audience, grew into

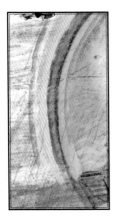

popular legends and were well known throughout Europe. How much the legendary journey is based on fact is of course unknown. It is possible that the *Navigatio* could have been written as early as the latter half of the eighth century, but even if we accept this as the date the Brendan legends were gathered and written down, this is still several hundred years after his death in 575. Over time storytellers will have embellished the adventures, and the various accounts that have been passed down to us today vary in their emphasis and style. In some we see Brendan's adventures retold as legends of a fantasy hero on a par with Odysseus. Others pay careful attention to the rhythm of a seven-year journey and use that to emphasize the importance of monastic tradition. But they all begin with Brendan sailing from Ireland on a journey of discovery to find a mythical promised land of the saints. Generally they all follow the same pattern and contain much the same adventures and, whether or not the voyage took place, as one continuous journey or as a conglomeration of many seafaring adventures, the *Navigatio* is a remarkable legend and has much with which to inspire and encourage its readers.

Brendan's heart had been captured by stories told by Barrind. This visiting abbot had told Brendan about a marvellous Eden-like land which could be found at the world's end and, that night, Brendan called fourteen monks from the abbey to his cell. He told them how much his heart had been stirred by Barrind's description and asked them whether they would join him on what would be a journey to the world's end, chasing paradise. Their response was to fast and pray and to ask God for his permission and blessing for their voyage. They knew all too well of the natural human response to become excited by an idea and be consumed by it, forgetting to consider whether the 'good thing' is also the 'right thing'. They knew that any decision should be put prayerfully before God to determine whether their plans were in line with his will. They knew also that God often uses natural human talents, and that Brendan was an accomplished sailor and the founding abbot of more than one monastery. They knew he takes account of the heart's desires, and Brendan clearly really wanted to go on this journey. The monks knew that all decisions had to be submitted to God, and that without his 'yes' they needed to be prepared to say no.

All this informed the answer of Brendan's monks: 'Abbot, your will is ours. Have we not left our parents behind? Have we not spurned our inheritance and given our bodies into your hands? So we are prepared to go along with you to death or life. Only one thing let us ask for, the will of God.' And so for forty days they fasted and prayed, taking time to visit neighbouring monasteries to speak with Brendan's friends and mentors, whose judgment they trusted. After this period of prayer they made ready a small wood and leather boat and set sail north, up the Atlantic coast around Ireland and Scotland.

During their journey Brendan and his crew landed at many dazzling islands, four of which they returned to each year in a rhythm that was inextricably linked to the church calendar. On

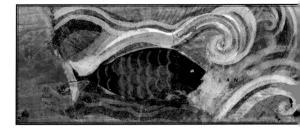

Maundy Thursday the band of men found themselves on the Island of the Steward. The steward was a young man who offered provision and guidance to the crew. The island is also known as the Island of the Sheep as flocks of white sheep that were larger than cattle covered the small isle. The steward gladly offered Brendan the pick of the flock for his feast as well as a spotless lamb to sacrifice.

As the feast of Easter approached the crew sighted land: a small stony island. The island was barren, a wasteland without tree or any kind of plant life. Upon landing, the monks, with the exception of Brendan who remained aboard the boat, set up their cooking pot and lit a small fire. No sooner was the fire lit than the rock they were standing on began to shake and before long the whole island was convulsing and moving quickly away from Brendan and the boat. The abbot calmly threw a line to his brothers and pulled the terrified monks back aboard. Brendan had remained on the boat having foreseen the situation in a dream, but why he then allowed the rest of his party to board what was actually a huge whale and light a fire, we can only guess. The Anglo-Norman version of the *Navigatio* though tells that his words to the terrified monks as he helped them back aboard the leather boat were: 'The more you see of his marvels the more firmly you will believe in Him'. Every year then, for the remainder of the voyage, the crew celebrated Easter on the back of Jasconius the whale, who became a friend and companion to the crew. He was often sighted swimming alongside their boat.

The next island the crew visited had an abundance of birds that seemed to join with the monks' daily rhythm of prayer and song. The *Navigatio* tells that one tree 'of extraordinary girth and no less height was covered with white birds. There were so many one could scarcely see its leaves or branches.' One of the birds settled on the boat next to Brendan and sang out to him, somehow explaining that these birds were angels that had fallen to earth from heaven and that they sang with constant praise to God. This angel – or bird – revealed to Brendan that he must continue to travel for seven years before returning to Ireland. The voyagers subsequently celebrated the feast of Pentecost on the Island of the Birds each year.

The final island marker was always reached just in time for Christmas. This island was home to a community of Christian monks who lived an isolated life of silence. The miraculous provision for these silent monks on their little island included a flaming arrow which sped in and out of an open window to light the candles in their chapel each evening before prayers.

During the regular cycle of islands that Brendan visited there were many adventures which broke up the rhythm of the voyage. After sailing for some days over an unusually clear sea the abbot sighted what we, in our age of encyclopedias and the Discovery Channel, would identify as a glacier. For these monks from the sixth century though, the first sighting of a 'pillar of bright crystal' filled them with awe and wonder. For several days they continued to sail towards the column which loomed larger and larger on the horizon. At last they drew close and with great seamanship Brendan navigated the boat around and into the interior of what they describe as a 'silver net' (layers of crystallized ice) that covered the crystal pillar. In 1976 a sailor by the name of Tim Severin retraced Brendan's epic voyage using a boat made from similar material to Brendan's. Severin too came close to a glacier and his terrifying description of sailing up to a colossal wall of ice that rose abruptly and dangerously from the sea is similar enough to the *Navigatio* to support the medieval voyager's account of travelling through an ice field.

Tim Severin's book *The Brendan Voyage* is a remarkable read and shows how many of the strange occurrences described by Brendan in the *Navigatio* could be based on fact. Brendan's tales tell of a coagulated sea in the Arctic Circle which Severin encountered as he travelled from Iceland to America. The modern sailor in his replica craft also experienced the Island of the Birds and the strange fog banks off the Canadian coast, just as the medieval monk had described. On another occasion Brendan's crew chanced upon what could possibly have been an erupting volcano. The *Navigatio* describes this as the 'Island of the Smiths' and tells how the crew saw huge angry blacksmiths hurl flaming rocks at the boat, chronicling how smoke billowed from the island.

As well as the adventures to mysterious and miraculous islands, Brendan's voyage also including meeting strangers. One of these was Judas, the betrayer of Christ, who the crew had found clinging to a rock battered by waves and wind. This, the sorry creature told them, was his weekly respite from hell. Each Saturday evening Judas was apparently chained to this rock and given the relief of near-drowning for a day. Judas pleaded with Brendan that he might be allowed an extra day of rest with which to celebrate the visit of the abbot. Brendan interceded for the man and the monks remained until demons came to retrieve their prize. In the tradition of Antony and other saints, Brendan spoke with authority to the demons, demanding that Judas be left for the extra day on his rock.

The other significant character Brendan came across was the Desert Father Paul of Thebe who was one of the original desert hermits. His biographer Jerome tells how Paul entered the desert as a hermit some years before Antony (of the Desert) and how the two venerated fathers met as old men at the end of Paul's life. Paul sent Antony away to fetch his cloak so as to spare Antony the grief of seeing his friend die. When Antony returned he found Paul dead, still on his knees in a posture of prayer, hands stretched out to heaven. Antony despaired at having nothing with which to dig a suitable grave for the man of God and in his grief failed to see two lions who came to help bury the hermit. During Brendan's voyage,

Paul is found naked except for the hair which covered his body so thickly that only his face and eyes could be seen. He had survived on this rocky island in his life of solitude thanks to an otter that for thirty years had brought the hairy hermit meals of fish and a regular supply of firewood. Paul greeted each of the monks by name and welcomed them. It was Paul who, at last, revealed to Brendan that his journey was nearing its conclusion and at the end of this round of island visits he would sail with the familiar steward for the 'promised land'.

And so it was from the first island that Brendan had visited – the Island of the Steward – that he made his final journey.

Brigid of Kildare

Adventure is not just about what you do in life – it's also about an attitude to life. Brigid, who died c. 525, may not have sailed into the unknown Atlantic but her life was full of adventure nonetheless. The story of Brigid is difficult to tell since legend surrounds her like a cloak, concealing fact with fiction.

Folklore holds that Brigid was the daughter of a Druid and that she was born in Leinster, Ireland. As she grew up she infuriated her father by giving away to the poor she met on the road anything that could be drunk, eaten or sold. The final straw came when Brigid gave away her father's valuable sword to a beggar. He had determined to sell Brigid at market but this last act of defiance persuaded him that she should be allowed to follow her own path into a nunnery.

Brigid was a defiant young lady and one can picture her standing on her chariot tearing about the countryside giving away provisions to the poor. One nobleman blockaded the road in an attempt to prevent her helping the peasants who lived on his land. Brigid simply looked for the weak point in the blockade and charged! The chariot didn't survive the crash but Brigid did – thus leaving us with the phrase 'Short cuts make for broken bones.'

Brigid later established the double monastery (double in the sense that both men and women were housed there) at Kildare and her legacy of female leadership in the Celtic Church was an example to many in the centuries that followed and indeed to us today.

After seven years of circling the same four islands it was the first person the travellers met on their voyage, the steward, that at last comes with Brendan as a guide. And it is only with the help of the steward that Brendan is able to find the island, for no matter how hard they searched they could not find their way alone. After a final forty days the boat landed on the coast of North America. Tim Severin's expedition landed in Newfoundland proving that such a journey was at least possible.

Other historians suggest that Brendan's final route took him south and that 'Brendan's Isle' is a Caribbean island. Until relatively recently 'Brendan's Isle' was marked on maps of the Atlantic Ocean. Christopher Columbus certainly read the *Navigatio* and this played its small part in firing the explorers' determination to sail beyond the known waters and eventually 'discover' the Americas nearly a thousand years after Brendan had landed.

The *Navigatio* doesn't linger long on the details of the island destination, nor on Brendan's return journey. But once again the author tells how the group were met by a young man who knew them by name and welcomed them to the island. The young man spoke to Brendan: 'There before you lies the land which you sought for a long time. You could not find it immediately because God wanted to show you his varied secrets of the ocean.' And there, with that sentence, we see the very essence of pilgrimage and of the *peregrinati*, the white martyrs; destination is always of secondary importance when compared to the journey. As a missionary and traveller I too have learned that often it is the journey that teaches us more than the destination, and in an 'instant age' we should try to value process as much as result. Just as Brendan had to circle his islands for seven long years, retracing his steps year after year, we often find ourselves on our own journeys repeating behaviour, visiting the same places time and again, never sure if we are really 'getting anywhere'. Brendan's journey, although a wonderful tale of adventure, is more about the journey of the soul. It is a journey where he learns, as we do, to trust and find faith. Brendan and his crew experienced danger, despair and loss as they journeyed each day into the unknown. Yet they were provided for and protected. The Anglo-Norman version of the *Navigatio* says:

> *Now the servants of God [Brendan and his brothers] perceived that they were journeying under God's direction; the miracles they had witnessed proved this beyond doubt. Seeing clearly that God would feed them, they never ceased praising Him and set off at once, sailing before the wind. God's protection was about them and for a good part of the year they sailed over the sea, suffering extreme hardship.*

Brendan's story shows that when people endure suffering, hardship, danger, despair and loss on their own voyages into their unknown tomorrows and they feel that their lives aren't going as they had hoped, this in no way means God has removed his protection or his blessing from them. More often the opposite is true; when people let go and abandon themselves to the guiding breath of God, his provision and protection can be found.

Brendan finally returned to Ireland where he continued to travel until old age, visiting northern France and Wales, helping to establish monasteries there. Finally he died in the arms of his beloved sister Scolastica at her abbey overlooking the Atlantic Ocean on which he had journeyed so far.

I first came across this poem or prayer from 'In exploration of a vision' in *Celtic Daily Prayer* by the Northumbria Community as my family and I prepared to leave our homeland and head off to live in Eastern Europe. It means a great deal to us and helps me to understand the Jesus that is with me in my sacrifice of home, career, will and desire; he is faithful and trustworthy and he will never let me go.

Lord I will trust you
Help me to journey beyond the familiar
And into the unknown.
Give me the faith to leave the old ways
And break new ground with You.
Christ of the mysteries, can I trust You
To be stronger than each storm in me?
I will trust in the darkness and know
That my times are still in your hand.
I will believe you for my future
Chapter by chapter until the story is written.
Strengthen me with Your blessing
And appoint me to the task.
Teach me to live with eternity in view.
Tune my spirit to the music in heaven.
Feed me,
And, somehow,
Make my obedience count for You.
Amen

CHAPTER 6

Celtic Saints
Learning and Discovery

Aidan, Abbot of Lindisfarne

> *Come to me, all you that are weary and are carrying*
> *heavy burdens, and I will give you rest. Take my yoke*
> *upon you, and learn from me; for I am gentle and*
> *humble in heart, and you will find rest for your souls.*
> *For my yoke is easy, and my burden is light.*
> Matthew 11:28–30

Two islands – one a mile or so off the west coast of Scotland, the other in the far north east of England – contributed more than any other place in the United Kingdom as it stands today to the Celtic evangelization of the British people.

It was to Iona that Columba, a fiery Irish priest, was sent to work amongst the Scots and the Picts. Some traditions recount the story that Columba was sent in exile from his homeland since he had been held responsible for a bloody battle which claimed many lives and was banished. He was subsequently charged

with winning for Christ as many men as had died in the battle.

Sailing away from his beloved homeland with a crew of twelve men, Columba set down at a number of islands on the western Scottish coast. But each time, as he looked back, he could still see Ireland in the distance and was compelled to sail further north. Eventually he landed on Iona, a small island which was in the shadow of the larger Isle of Mull. Here he established a monastery and worked amongst the people of Northumbria. From Iona, missionary monks were sent further south through England and onto the continent.

Then came the story of Lindisfarne – also known as Holy Island – and in many ways this story sums up the Celtic Church. The community served the populace, working as they did in all areas of society, from the royal courts to the slaves they saved from the markets. They sought to educate and bring skills to the people, and they purposefully spread their gospel message across all the tribes: across the Picts (an ancient tribe from the region known today as the Scottish Highlands), the Scots, the Angles and the Britons. And so we see that on Lindisfarne, there was not a single radical community but one of many different inhabitants of different social groups living in close proximity of each other and coming together in various ways, in the model of the Celtic way. They cared for the people and the land; they valued the arts and music and they travelled farther and farther afield in an attempt to deliver the gospel. The Celtic Church has a great deal to teach us about prayer and contemplation in seclusion, but it was also a church that demonstrated the love of Jesus in action as much as reflection. There is a lovely anecdote that came from the Desert Fathers but also seems to aptly summarize the Celtic Church:

*A brother asked one of the elders: 'There are two
brothers of whom one remains in his cell, fasting six
days at a time and doing a great deal of penance. The
other takes care of the sick. Which one's work is more
pleasing to God?'*

*The Elder replied: 'If that brother who fasts six
days at a time were to hang himself up by the nose –
he could not equal the one who cares for the sick.'*

The Celtic model is one that prefers to walk amongst the people
as Jesus did. The Celts saw the gospel of Jesus as a message for
individuals that transcended the barriers of class and society.
While they didn't shy away from working with the rich and
powerful, they were just as comfortable walking through the
fields and living with the lowliest in their society. And just as
we can see so many other Celtic communities in the DNA of
Lindisfarne, when we look at the island's first abbot, Aidan, we
see in him the example of many other Celtic saints, both those
like Columba, whose example he would have learned from, and
those whose lives he impacted on and followed in the generations
after he lived.

The story of Aidan and Lindisfarne begins in more than one
way on Iona for it is on Iona that Aidan first heard his call from
God and made the decision to go to the remote place that was
Lindisfarne. But more than that, as with so much Celtic history,
this is a story surrounded by echoes and shadows.

Some years before Aidan's call, Oswald, king of Northumbria,
had been exiled to Iona and was educated there by the monks.
In AD 633 or 634 Oswald triumphed in the historic Battle of
Heavenfield, winning back Northumbria from the British king,

Cadwalla. King Oswald dedicated the victory to God, promising to see his people have the same education he himself had received on Iona. He also wanted to have his kingdom evangelized.

Oswald's appeal for missionary teachers was heard and responded to by the local community. A monk by the name of Corman was sent across from Iona to Bamburgh in Northumbria. How Corman came to have been chosen we don't know. Equally we can't know how long he spent in Northumbria before we see him again on Iona. But we do know that Corman's return to Iona coincided with a visit from Aidan.

A council had been called to hear Corman's report on his attempts to evangelize Northumbia. There must have been some disappointment amongst the people to see the monk back so soon and as the council sat listening to his story, Corman's body language must have given away his anger and frustration. Corman was embarrassed because he had failed his task. A short while ago, he had been chosen, or had volunteered, to embark on an exciting voyage to take the gospel message into a new land. But he had not been able to complete what he had set out to do. Corman angrily told the council that it was no use, that these people were too difficult: they were stubborn men who were uncivilized and cruel.

One can picture Aidan sitting and listening quietly at the back of the room. Every insult about the Northumbrian people was a challenge. The more Corman dismissed them as barbaric the more Aidan's heart warmed towards them. Eventually Aidan could take no more. As the rest of the room sat in stunned silence the tall, strong Irish monk stood and raised his voice: 'Methinks, brother, that you were more severe to your unlearned hearers than you ought to have been, and did not at first, conformably to the apostolic rule, give them the milk of more easy doctrine, till, being by degrees nourished with the Word of God, they should be capable of receiving that which is more perfect and of performing the higher precepts of God.' He hadn't meant to say anything; this wasn't his plan. He certainly had no intention prior to the council of taking Corman's place in this 'barbaric' land – he already had his own community in Ireland. And yet, as is often the way, as his heart softened, he found himself being volunteered to replace Corman.

Arriving in Northumbria in AD 635, Aidan wasn't alone in this strange land. As well as the company of twelve men he had chosen from the community on Iona, King Oswald was to become a magnificent ally and friend to the new community. Oswald began by offering Aidan any land he liked from within the kingdom. He was welcome too to stay within the castle at Bamburgh and use that as his base. However Aidan, knowing the teaching of Columba, required that his monastery should 'be alone in a separate place near a chief city'. The proximity to the city, where Christians should serve and influence, as well as the distance which would allow a degree of separation and space for contemplation, were equally important. Aidan could not then stay within the castle nor could he be too far removed from the centre of Northumbrian power. The obvious answer was a tidal island just a couple of miles away from the town. It wasn't a large island but it was perfectly suited to the community's needs. More importantly, the fact that the island was tidal meant that twice a day it was possible to walk or ride to and from the mainland. This gave the monks the contact they needed while still protecting their solitude.

Oswald was to prove more than a benevolent benefactor, and in his work *The Ecclesiastical History of the English People*, the venerable Bede called him a 'most Christian King'. Bede went to some length to record his good deeds in life as well as a fair few miraculous signs which followed his death and helped with the king's later sanctification. Oswald became one of the first recorded English saints. In fact, Bede records how the king himself humbly acts as translator for the monks as they travelled the region before they had learned the local language.

Another account tells the tale of how one cold night Aidan and others were called to feast at the king's table. A servant sheepishly appeared and told the king that a group of beggars was at the door asking for food. The king, without hesitation, took the roasted meat from the table telling the servant to share it amongst the people. As the servant turned to leave the king appeared to change his mind. 'Wait!' he called out. 'Take the silver platter the meat is served on. Have them share the profit amongst them.' Aidan who sat quietly witnessing the king's generosity was overcome with joy. He took the king's hand and blessed him for his piety, saying, 'May this hand never wither.'

Oswald was later killed in battle by Penda, the notorious and evil king of Mercia. After Oswald's death, Penda had Oswald's hands and head mounted on stakes, but when Oswald's brother, Oswy, rode out in a daring mission to capture Penda's trophies, Bede tells how the hands and head had miraculously been preserved. After the death of Oswald the Northumbrian kingdom was divided between Oswy and Oswald's cousin, Oswin.

Aidan and Oswin became firm friends and the king regularly visited Holy Island, although he always made sure he left before the evening meal so as not to be a drain on the island's resources. On one occasion, after Aidan had spent an evening

in the king's company, Oswin announced he had a gift for the community. He rose and Aidan followed. As they walked Oswin explained how he had seen the bishop often walk through his land journeying for many days by foot, travelling to outlying towns and settlements. This was no way for a bishop to travel, he said. Aidan of course argued that the place for the church and its servants is always amongst the people; walking with them rather than in the lofty position of a rider who can pass by without noticing what is going on around him. Nevertheless when the time came and they reached the stables it was not in Aidan's power to decline the gift the king showed him. To have refused would have been an insult, for the king had chosen his best horse and saddled it with the finest silver and leather harness. It is easy to imagine Oswin standing proudly offering such a fine gift, a horse and its saddle – all of which would have been worth a small fortune at the time. Aidan thanked the king for his kindness, his thoughts and his generosity; but at the same time he was not at all sure how he should react at being given such a valuable gift. Aidan practised poverty and took no possessions for himself so how then could he reconcile this with owning such a beast? He put these thoughts temporarily behind him as he thanked his friend and took to the saddle for the ride home. How was he going to explain this back on the island?

Aidan smiled to himself as he thought of how he would be greeted by his friends when he returned on horseback, and what a horse! And yet he knew that it could not last. Travelling by horseback would, of course, save them all a lot of time. But a rider was elevated above those around them and above the countryside through which he travelled. This meant that he missed out on so much in the company of others and the blessings of nature. What a lesson this is for the twenty-first century! How much do we miss out on each day by travelling at the speeds that modern cars, planes and trains afford? Could we learn from Aidan and slow down once in a while? I'm sure our days would be greatly enriched if we were able to do so.

But Aidan didn't get very far on his horse. Passing through the town gates he heard the voice of a beggar and the bishop, of course, stopped to talk. Climbing down from the horse he began to offer the man kindness and a blessing. Then he stopped. He looked at the horse, then at the poor man with his empty begging bowl, then back at the horse. He smiled, then began to laugh. Here was the answer! How could a man hold onto such a valuable possession when those around him had nothing? The rule of Columba says it is not fitting for a religious man to have any distinction of property with his brother. Aidan held the horse's face close and whispered a goodbye, then took the reigns, handing them with a bow and a smile to the beggar man.

The story of Aidan and the horse does not end there. Aidan still had to face the king and explain what he had done with his gift. He didn't have to wait long. The king soon requested the company of the bishop at a hunting banquet. Oswin must have heard what had happened, for this is, after all a small town in a small kingdom and it was the business of the king to know the comings and goings of his people.

Aidan waited for the king and the noblemen of the hunting
party to return to the banqueting hall. As the king strode into
the room Aidan rose and moved to greet his friend. King Oswin,
however, refused to meet the bishop's embrace. 'What do you
mean, my lord bishop, by giving the poor man a royal horse?
Had I known what you would do with such a fine beast I would

have chosen something more fitting! I gave you my very best.' Aidan looked Oswin in the eye. 'My king, my good friend. Is the son of a mare more dear to you than that son of God?' The king turned his back and remained warming himself by the fire for some time as Aidan and the rest of the guests moved towards the table. Eventually he turned and knelt before the bishop. 'Forgive me Aidan. I will never again question what you choose to do with a gift of mine. I will not judge you for what you give to the sons of God. And I will never again speak of this.'

Later as the meal continued the bishop grew quiet. With concern, his priest asked what was wrong. The bishop, through thinly disguised tears, said: 'I fear,' speaking in his native Scottish tongue so as not to be overheard, 'that the king will not live long.' He spoke plainly though with a weight of sadness. 'For I never before saw such a humble king and I fear the that this nation is not worthy of such a ruler.'

It wasn't long before Aidan's prophetic words came true. Oswy sought to unite Northumbria and to do this he needed Oswin out of the way. The two armies were roused but on the day of the battle, seeing that he was hopelessly outnumbered and not willing to commit his men to their death, Oswin disbanded his army and fled the field. He took refuge in a friend's house, but was betrayed and eventually assassinated. Aidan was heartbroken and twelve days later collapsed on his way into the church at Bamburgh. He never recovered and died on the threshold of the church he loved in 651.

As is typical of the synchronicity we often see in the Celtic Church, at the time when Aidan whispered his final prayer, a young shepherd was out on the hills of Northumbria. As he sat on that still night in late August he saw a vision which gripped

Hild, Abbess of Whitby

The story of Hild (or Hilda) is entwined within the history of Northumbria at the time of Aidan. She was born in AD 614 and, as the great niece of King Edwin, was baptized by the Italian bishop Paulinus. In addition, she was cousin to both Oswald and Oswy.

Hild was baptized at an early age and desired more than anything to enter the monastic life. At the time Aidan had prepared only a place for men in the communities of Northumbria. Hild wanted the education and the life that a monastery would give her and seeing the lack of provision for nunneries in her homeland, she set out for France. There were many monastic communities for women abroad and she intended to enter a community near Paris. On her way, she stopped off to visit her family in East Anglia and it was there that she received a letter from Aidan. He had had a change of heart and implored her not to leave England and instead return to her native Northumbria to help him with the evangelization of the region.

Hild not only became abbess of Hartlepool Abbey in Northumbria but also founded the double monastery of Whitby. Such was her prominence within the church that she was the host of the Council of Whitby which pitched the Roman church and tradition against that of the Celts. St Wilfrid and the Romans won the argument and the church in England was compelled thereafter to follow their tradition. Colman who had led the Celtic delegation couldn't stand to see his beloved Celtic Church become subject to the Roman Pattern and left for Iona. It says much for Hild's love of her country that she chose to remain at Whitby despite the new regime. And it was Hild who encouraged Caedmon at Whitby to sing the narrative of the Bible in English which until then had been considered a pagan language unfit for ecclesiastical use. She died in 680.

him and changed for ever the path of his life. In his vision he saw countless angels descending from heaven to the town not far from where he watched over the sheep. Then as the angels ascended they took with them a great light. The next day, as the young man learnt of the death of the bishop Aidan, he made the decision to dedicate his life to God and the church. This young man's name was Cuthbert and he later stood in the line of Aidan as abbot of Lindisfarne, emulating the pioneering bishop and continuing the work he had begun.

David Adams's biography of Aidan entitled *Flame In My Heart* closes with this prayer which cries out to God asking that the example of Aidan – his character, his love for others and the light that he was to the un-evangelized Northumbrians – might speak to people today:

> *Lord God who called Aidan to burn like a flame in*
> *the dark ages, set our hearts on fire with your love,*
> *open our eyes to your glory, open our lives to your*
> *brightness, and help us to show forth your light today;*
> *through Christ our Lord, who is the Light of the*
> *world, and reigns with you and the Holy Spirit, for*
> *ever more.*
> *Amen*

CHAPTER 7

Eastern Saints
Wisdom and Grace

Cyril and Methodius

> *To the weak I became weak, so that I might win the weak. I have become all things to all people, so that I might by any means save some. I do it all for the sake of the gospel, so that I may share in its blessings.*
> 1 Corinthians 9:22, 23

Today Moravia is a part of eastern Czech Republic. It is a small province that was once much grander than it is now. 'Great' Moravia covered much of central Europe, extending to the north into Germany and Poland, and south as far as Serbia and Bosnia and Herzegovina. To the west it reached into modern day Italy and east it stretched as far as Romania. Moravia was 'great' for a relatively short period towards the end of the first millennium. Then, as with so many lesser empires of the Middle Ages it

diminished in size and stature due to internal power struggles and external wars with its many neighbours. Finally Moravia became absorbed and annexed into the rising Slovak and Magyar (Hungarian) territories.

Despite this, Moravia has left a sizeable footprint on the history of the Christian church in Europe. By the time of the eighteenth century, the Moravian Church had become largely responsible for the modern missions movement and most, if not all, Christian mission organizations today trace their roots back to the mission-minded Moravian Church. John Wesley, the founder of the Methodist church, was so impressed by the Moravians he met on his voyage to America in 1735 that on his return he allied himself with the movement.

It was reformer and clergyman Jan Hus (John Huss), c. 1370–1415, who laid the foundations that gave birth to the modern Moravian Church. His desire to see a simpler church, accessible to all and with the liturgy in the language of the layman rather than in Latin – which none but the most elite could understand – eventually led to him being burnt at the stake. And yet, over 500 years earlier, the first missionaries to Great Moravia had already done exactly what he fought for; not only had they translated the gospel into the local Slavic language but they had also created a written form of the language in order to do so. They introduced a Slavic liturgy and despite huge opposition won the approval of Rome. The leaders of this small band of missionary brothers were cited by Pope John Paul II for their advancement of the gospel and for their desire to bring unity to the catholic (holy and universal) church.

Cyril (827–69) and Methodius (826–85), as patron saints of Europe, are today honoured for their role in shaping the church across this continent. That they are venerated in both the Orthodox and Catholic traditions speaks of the tremendous work Cyril and Methodius did in bridging the widening schism that was appearing in their age between the church of the East and that of the West.

Cyril, who was originally known as Constantine, was born the youngest son to a noble family in the bustling metropolis seaport of Thessaloniki in present-day Greece. His father was a high-ranking commander in the Byzantine army; his mother was probably of Slavic descent and theirs was a family of prominence in the upper social circles in this corner of the Byzantine empire. Being located as they were on the fringes of the Slavic nations, on the southern edge of ancient Macedonia, Cyril and his brother Methodius would have spoken Slavic, in addition to Greek. When their father died the brothers were teenagers and they were entrusted to their uncle, a very well-connected figure in the Byzantine empire. Their education could not have been in better hands; indeed it was this kind uncle who, a few years later, was responsible for education reforms across the empire.

The brothers graduated from the University of Constantinople and Methodius became the abbot of a well-known monastery on Mount Olympus. Meanwhile, Cyril was installed as librarian for the patriarch Photius and taught philosophy at his old university. Cyril, with a missionary's zeal and a wandering spirit, was later selected as an envoy to the Saracens. This was probably more to do with political and trade relations than an evangelistic expedition, but it served to foster a desire to take the Christian message into the world beyond the Byzantine boundaries. And so in 861 Cyril was sent by the emperor to the Khazars who occupied much of southern Russia. It was during this journey that Cyril discovered the remains of an ancient saint, Clement of Rome, in a small church. Recognizing these remains were a hugely significant artefact for the church, Cyril carried them with him, first back to Constantinople, then on a later mission before making a gift of them to the church in Rome.

Then in 863 came the cry from the new prince of Moravia, Ratislav: 'Many Christian teachers have reached us from Italy, from Greece and from Germany, who instruct us in different ways. But we Slavs are simple people and have no one to direct us towards the truth and instruct us in an understandable way.' Who could help? Who understood the Slavic ways and their language enough to incarnate the gospel in that culture? The Byzantine emperor Michael III appealed to Cyril, 'Do you hear these words, philosopher? None but you can go.'

Cyril's responses were 'However tired and physically worn out I am; I will go with joy to that land' and 'With joy I depart for the sake of the Christian faith'. He may have only recently returned from his adventures in the east, so the prospect of leaving again so soon, once again to a distant foreign land, may not have appealed. Perhaps this is why Methodius joined him: to take care of his younger brother.

Having heard the call from the emperor, the brothers devoted themselves to prayer. In their prayers for the Slavs they asked God for strategy and more than anything, a way to teach the gospel to these 'simple people'. This was a problem of literacy

at its most basic; these people couldn't read – and their language, Slavic, had no written form. One account says:

> *They turned to the Comforter and begged of him this grace: to invent an alphabet that might contain the wildness of the Bulgarian language. They begged Him for the ability to translate the divine scriptures into the tongue of that people… and they received that for which they yearned.*

And so it was that God revealed the Slavic script to Cyril in a vision. Armed with this new alphabet which encapsulated 'the wildness' of the Slavic language and a gospel message in the new script, they began their mission.

We know that at least two other men formed part of the team that Cyril and Methodius led. There was Clement, a young Slavic scholar, and Naum. The icons we have become accustomed to seeing depict these saints as elderly men with bald heads and astonishingly long grey beards, but on leaving Macedonia the youngest of the band, Clement, would have been just twenty-three years old, and as the eldest, Methodius would have been about forty! There certainly weren't too many grey hairs among them when they set out. However, iconography allows for the use of imagery and more often the depiction of a long grey beard would be used to show the saint as a wise man. Indeed, many Eastern icons depict saints with over-large, bulbous heads which look strange to our modern Western eyes, but would convey an understanding of assumed wisdom to those in the ancient Eastern church.

In the spring of 863 the band of men left the relative comfort of their monastic and academic lives and began their journey northwards. Travelling from Constantinople along the Danube and Tisa rivers they found their way blocked and were unable to enter Moravia due to an invasion of Germanic tribes. War barred their entry, but instead of seeing this as a setback, the brothers began evangelizing the Rus tribes of the Carpathian Mountains and before they left a year later they had already instated a bishop and several priests to care for their converts!

Even dismissing the way war blocked their path it would seem that Methodius at least wasn't the greatest of travelling companions. Clement writes of the leader, that 'all along his travels the devil sent him abundant scourges: in the wilderness, robbers; in the sea, storms and tempests; on the rivers, sudden sandy shallows...' It is not surprising then to learn that their journey to Moravia took a year!

Cyril and Methodius's mission to Moravia was a success despite much opposition from within the Western church. The archbishop of Salzburg, who claimed control over Moravia, was furious at the brothers' use of Slavic liturgy in services and of their translation of the Bible into Slavic. Accused of heresy, Pope Nicholas I invited the brothers to Rome to defend themselves in 867.

Cyril though was skilled in the art of debate and easily won the approval and blessing of the pope. He had argued:

Do not all breathe the air in the same way? And you are not ashamed to decree only three languages (Hebrew, Greek and Latin); deciding that all other peoples and races should remain blind and deaf! Tell me: do you hold this because you consider God is so weak that he cannot grant it, or so envious that he does not wish it?

This is quite incredible when we consider the arguments put forward by Cyril as the backdrop to the Reformation which was to take place 500 years later. Sadly though the younger brother was never to return to the mission field he loved. Taken by illness, he died in Rome in 869. On his death bed Cyril prayed, 'Hear my prayer and protect your faithful people, for you have established me as their unsuitable and unworthy servant.' Unsuitable and unworthy? This Greek who became a Slav for the sake of the gospel, who was responsible for the evangelization and education of not just one country but an entire people group?

Having prayed he called his brother to him, 'Behold, my brother, we have shared the same destiny, ploughing the same furrow; I now fall in the field at the end of my day. I know that you greatly love your Mountain; but do not for the sake of the Mountain give up your work of teaching. For where better can you find salvation?' On his deathbed Cyril was calling his brother back to the mission field of Moravia; to leave his mountain, Rome, and return to care for the Slavs God had entrusted to them.

The opposition that first brought the brothers to Rome was to plague Methodius for the rest of his life. He was constantly accused and then cleared of heresy. At one point he was cruelly imprisoned for two and a half years. It took the intervention of Pope John VIII to free Methodius whereupon he was brought to Rome, again, to answer the charges against him. Once more Methodius was cleared of all charges and then embraced by the pope. Finally he was raised to the status of archbishop and sent to Moravia under papal orders; this was effectively a 'to whom it may concern' letter, confirming Methodius was sent by the pope and that people should stop harassing the poor man!

Methodius dedicated the rest of his life to the spreading of the gospel in central Europe. It was a gospel that was made accessible for the 'simple man' and one that was woven into the Slavic life. Following his death in 885 the opposition that Cyril and Methodius's followers faced became outright persecution. Faced with beatings and imprisonment most fled the country but in so doing spread their work far wider than if they were to have stayed in Moravia.

Today the Cyrillic alphabet is widely used across the south east of Europe, throughout Russia and also the ex-Soviet states. The legacy of Cyril and Methodius though goes far beyond the linguistic heritage they left behind. These were men gave up their positions in society, turned their backs on promising careers and instead gave their lives to helping others, living and dying as foreigners in a strange land. These saints are an example in humility and in obedience to the call of God. They sacrificed all they had to see the Christian message lived out in words and action, deliberately stepping around the popular arguments of the day which were intent on splitting the church – and instead reached out with this same humility to the Western and Eastern churches. In the words of Pope John Paul II, 'We salute the eleventh centenary of Saint Methodius's death... he gave an example of a vocation fruitful not only for the century in

Clement of Ohrid

Looking back across Macedonia's Lake Ohrid to the town of the same name, it is possible to clearly see the church of St John perched on top of the cliffs to the west of the old town. Just above this church and hidden from view is another church. This one has been restored in recent years and now houses the relics of St Clement of Ohrid. The church is dedicated to Saints Clement and Pantelejmon and stands on or near the site of what some call the first university in Europe.

Clement (840–916) was a Slav from southern Macedonia who was a disciple of Cyril and Methodius. Along with St Naum he relocated to Ohrid after they were forced to flee Moravia in the backlash of persecution following Methodius's death.

Clement was invested as bishop of Ohrid, becoming the first Slav to be given that title. From the Ohrid area, Clement and Naum continued the work of Cyril and Methodius, refining further the written alphabet. It is likely that it was Clement who named the alphabet 'Cyrillic' in honour of his teacher. In establishing a significant literary school, Naum and Clement played a large part in the ongoing evangelization of the eastern Balkans, Russia and its surrounding territories and tribes, sending over 2,500 missionaries out from this small Macedonian town. With Clement and Naum at the helm, the hills surrounding Ohrid were littered with a great number of monasteries. It is thought that at one time there were 364 monasteries and churches in the area around Lake Ohrid – that's nearly one for each day of the year!

which he lived but also for the centuries which followed, and in a special way for our own times.'

John of Damascus, (675–749) or John Damascene, as he is also known, was a Doctor of the Church; a great writer and thinker. His works helped and influenced many, but it is perhaps the tenderness of his poetry that leaves an even greater mark. In this short poem-prayer, the 'Hymn to the Life-Giving Cross', John wonderfully captured the fragile nature of humankind and the redemptive nature of God.

Ceaselessly we bow, O Christ our God,
Before your cross that gives us life,
And glorify your resurrection,
Most powerful Lord,
When on that day you made anew
The failing nature of humankind,
Showing us so clearly
The way back to heaven above:
For you alone are good,
The Lover-of-Humankind.

CHAPTER **8**

Poor Saints
Beauty and Creativity

Francis of Assisi

Then he [Jesus] said to them all, 'If any want to become my followers, let them deny themselves and take up their cross daily and follow me. For those who want to save their life will lose it, and those who lose their life for my sake will save it. What does it profit them if they gain the whole world, but lose or forfeit themselves? Those who are ashamed of me, and of my words, of them the Son of Man will be ashamed when he comes in his glory and the glory of the Father and of the holy angels.'
Luke 9:23–26

The picture of the Christian church at the end of its first thousand years is rather different from that which we painted with the stories of Polycarp and the Early Church Fathers at its inception.

Christianity was no longer the religion of a persecuted minority and had not been so for 700 years. Ever since Charlemagne had been enthroned as leader of the new Christian (Holy Roman) empire in 800, the bishop of Rome had in effect become the leader of all Christendom, more powerful even than the emperor himself. Papal authority did not extend to appointing kings and emperors but they could certainly have had them removed if they wished and it was the pope who was required to anoint and, in so doing, validate a newly installed monarch. Without this blessing a fresh-faced king would not be expected to last long.

This was the era of the powerful crusading church. The years from 1095 to 1250 have been marked as one of the darkest periods in the Christian faith. The First Crusade to retake Jerusalem had been called for by Pope Urban II who took a 'just war' philosophy far further than had ever been intended. By the end of the Fifth Crusade the concept had been so mutilated by successive Roman pontiffs that Crusades were being launched within Christendom to combat heretical movements as well as battling Muslims in the Near East and Africa.

But the church at this time wasn't completely without hope. There were within the life of St Francis several senior church figures who helped to steer the young man and cared enormously for his well being; sometimes they may have taken their fatherly responsibility too far but these were good men who followed God and cared for their people.

Francis was born on the cusp of a new age in 1181. The Dark Ages had drawn to a close and the faintest glimmer of a new dawn, the dawn of the renaissance, was beginning to light the horizon. It was a time of war, bloodshed and brutality. But for some the High Middle Ages were also a time of prosperity. The arts were beginning to flourish, trade routes were increasingly bringing luxuries to the marketplace. Capitalism was spreading and merchants were moving up in the world. Francis's father Pietro Bernadone was such a merchant – a trader in expensive cloth and an astute businessman who worked hard and enjoyed a good amount of success. He traded in the finest and most fashionable of dyed fabric and was often travelling abroad.

Francis's mother Pica is remembered as a devout lady. Her son was born while her husband Pietro was out of town, but she went ahead and had Francis quickly baptized. During the Middle Ages more than half of all children died before they reached six months' old and only a fraction made it to adulthood. She was therefore not only following tradition but also assuring her son's salvation should he not survive the coming months. Pica christened her child Giovanni (John) after John the Forerunner (or John the Baptist as he is otherwise known).

Pietro was furious at his wife's choice of name for his son and heir. As far as he was concerned Pica had chosen to name their child after a vagrant prophet who dressed in rags and ate locusts – someone who was little more than a madman! The child was the heir to Pietro's precious name and business, and should therefore have had a title that impressed and also suited the image he would be expected to portray. Pietro intervened and from that moment Giovanni (John) became known as Francesco (Francis).

It is worth pausing a moment in our story to consider the nature of the chosen names. In doing so we may see and understand something more of the later life and character of St Francis. They were perhaps a foreshadow.

With the profit of hindsight, we can look back at the life of Francis and clearly see the 'Giovanni' in him; that is the character of John the Forerunner – of John the Baptist – the last prophet and herald of Jesus Christ; the man who preached 'Prepare!' and 'Make straight the paths'. Francis was a prophet who stirred the establishment of his day, especially the established church. Other monastic movements were impressed by his message and learned from him and so society too was perhaps softened and changed by his example.

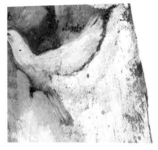

But Francis was also 'Francesco' – 'the Frenchman'. He was the charismatic charmer, a troubadour who led people by example into foolishness. The English writer G. K. Chesterton referred to him as 'Le Jongleur de Dieu' – 'The Jester of God' – for he was flamboyant and carefree at least in so much as he cared not a jot for what people thought of him.

So here we have the boy of a pious mother who becomes the wandering prophet and the father's son who is the centre of attention, the witty minstrel and the captivating preacher. Neither of these descriptions or even the patchwork combination image does justice to the true Francis of Assisi. His example in servanthood, his attitude to self, to creation and its Creator, this all shouts loud and clear from Francis's life and deserves to be heard and considered as relevant and poignant in the twenty-first century. Today we struggle to find the face of a true servant, rightly praising exceptions like Mother Teresa who are so rare.

As the son of a successful merchant Francis would have been expected not only to take his place working at the shop learning the family trade, but also to accompany his father as he travelled to the important fairs in Europe. He would have experienced life on the road, mixing with other merchants as well as rougher elements, perhaps mercenaries and soldiers on the way to or from a crusade. Certainly he would have spent time being entertained by travelling jugglers, acrobats, minstrels, storytellers and street fighters who all made a living on the road. Francis had plenty of stories and songs to bring back to Assisi, and he was the centre of his band of friends as they dreamed and schemed after hearing his tales of returning crusaders. The dream of the day was of course to become a knight, earning fame and fortune in battle, preferably in 'Holy War'.

At the age of sixteen Francis and his friends got a chance to try out their dream. It may not have been the chance of knighthood – there would be plenty of time for that – and it certainly wasn't a crusade in some exotic land, but it was at least the chance to fight. The dukedoms as well as the towns of Italy were embroiled in a more or less constant battle for supremacy. These wars were no less brutal or indeed fatal than those fought on foreign soil and in this particular battle against Assisi's neighbouring town of Perugia, hundreds of men were killed.

While taking part in this battle, Francis was taken captive and imprisoned with little food, no clean drinking water and with no means of sanitation. In spite of his situation he is said to have remained high spirited and served as the entertainer amongst his fellow prisoners of war. After nearly a year in captivity his parents paid a ransom for his release. Aside from the mental scarring such a period of confinement left on the young man, Francis had also contracted malaria during his imprisonment. It was a disease which was to plague him for the rest of his life. For most of the year after his release Francis was confined to his sick bed, barely leaving the house as the malaria brought with it fever, shivers and delirium to his young body.

Eventually Francis did recover. He perhaps emerged a shade more melancholy than he had been before, but he was still the boastful young leader of the pack he had always been. He continued to work for his father and continued to dream of knighthood. But although externally little had changed he was showing internally something of a new concern for the poor. Perhaps this was due to the image of the gallant prince he so wanted to portray or maybe God was slowly softening his heart. His concern is illustrated by the story of how one day while working in his father's shop a man came to the door begging for food. Francis was busy with a customer and seemed to ignore the poor man who shuffled away hungry. But as soon as the business was concluded Francis tore out the door and ran down the busy street shouting after the beggar. Eventually out of breath Francis found the man and thrust money into his grateful hand.

Although still weak from malaria Francis was a bored young adolescent who needed more than life as a merchant of Assisi could bring him. So, at the first opportunity, Francis again joined a cause. He bought new armour and the most extravagant costume which had been fashioned from his father's most expensive cloth and rode from Assisi with another group of friends, once again to join the fight.

This time our young hero didn't make it much further than the town boundary. His malaria flared up and he once again became seriously ill. As he burnt with fever beside the road he heard a voice: 'Francis. Who can do more for you, the servant or the master?' When he awoke, besides being in no condition to travel, Francis knew that in order to follow 'the master' he must return to Assisi and as he made his way home Francis overtook a leper. Lepers in the Middle Ages weren't just outcasts, they were feared and loathed by a society who couldn't understand the disease and often saw it as God's judgment on the wicked with lepers being made by law to carry a bell to warn people of their approach. Leprosy was untreatable and caused the flesh to die, slowly. Extremities were disfigured as the flesh withered and dying from leprosy was a long and lonely process. Francis's natural reaction was one of panic and with a sharp intake of breath he spurred the horse to speed past the hooded figure. Something though stopped him, he looked back, and trembling with fear and not without a little repulsion walked up to the man, looked him in the eyes and threw his arms around him. It was a brief embrace which meant more symbolically to both men than the awkward act. Then Francis stepped back and thrust all the money he had into the man's withered hand. It was another marker in the life of Francis and in his conversion story.

As Francis once again lay recovering at his parents' house he had time to reflect and consider. Later, as he walked the hills around the town he took time to think and to pray. Occasionally he would visit the decrepit chapel of San Damiano not far from Assisi and sit on the cool flagstone floor staring at the church's only decoration, a simple crucifix. It was during one of his visits to San Damiano that Francis heard the words that sent his whole life on an alternate course. This is the crux of what is a long conversion story. When Peter the disciple received his instruction from Jesus to 'Feed my sheep' in John 21:17 it had been preceded with the triple question 'Do you love me?' As Francis lay down and placed his face on the floor before the altar he heard Jesus speak instruction and commission into his life. But the question 'Do you love me?' had been asked over and over again during the preceding weeks and months: as he sat comforting friends in the prison Jesus had asked 'Do you love me?'; when he met the leper on the road Jesus asked 'Do you love me?' and then as Francis spent time walking alone in the hills of Assisi Jesus asked 'Do you really love me?' each time building up to this moment of faith. 'Francis,' called the voice. 'Do you see my house is in ruins? Go then and rebuild it for me.'

This then was Francis's instruction and was to remain his mission for the rest of his life, that is, 'to rebuild the church'. Francis obediently assumed a literal application tackling the restoration of the decrepit chapel of San Damiano. Later this physical application gave way to or was overtaken by the spiritual as Francis and the Franciscan movement became a force for regeneration in the Catholic Church.

Straight away Francis set about the building work for the chapel and the first place he turned to for help was his father, or rather his father's business and his money. Francis took fabric and sold it to raise the money he needed to buy stone and building material. The church refused the money but the damage had been done. Pietro was furious for his son had stolen, cheated and evidently gone quite mad. He dragged Francis back to Assisi, locked him up and eventually brought him before the bishop in the ecclesiastical court.

Francis could make no defence against his father and gave back all the money he had stolen. He then asked for a moment. To the bemusement of the crowd, his father and the bishop, Francis slipped into a side room and a short time later, he strode back into the chamber, naked, carrying his clothes in a tight ball in front of him. We should remember that there was little social concern around nudity in the Middle Ages and yet Pietro was more than embarrassed of his son – he was ashamed. Francis was publicly disowning him. Standing naked before the bishop Francis swore, 'Up until this day Pietro Bernadone has been my father. From this moment I have only our Father who art in heaven.' Pietro stormed from the scene leaving his son cold, naked and alone in the centre of the room. As Francis watched his father walk away and carve a path through the crowd he knew he was more alone than he had ever been. The bishop Guido was quick to react and at once enveloped Francis in his great ecclesiastical cloak shielding him in what was a wonderful symbol of the church taking and holding the vulnerable youngster, protecting him from the judgment of watchful eyes.

Walking away from the town of Assisi that day Francis had walked into his life of devotion to Christ and of service to humanity. He made his home a local church; the floor was his bed. Later, when he moved to a ruined cattle shed he was quickly joined by others who were attracted to his vow of poverty and simplicity.

One of the first of the brothers to join Francis was a rich young man by the name of Bernard of Quintaville. Bernard brought with him a purse of money which was his inheritance. This money was quickly spent, or given away in their efforts to restore the church. One day, as Francis was paying for building material, the priest Sylvester pushed his way through the small crowd and demanded attention. Francis had begged stone from him before Bernard's arrival and Sylvester was far from happy at seeing others recompensed for stone he had given for free. Having patiently heard the mumbled complaints of the priest Francis knelt at his feet and taking two full handfuls of coins pressed them with thanks into the priest's hands. The wonderful end to this little story is that several weeks later Sylvester, wracked with guilt and so impressed by Francis's example, returned and asked forgiveness, which goes without saying was freely given. Sylvester thus became another welcome addition to the growing band of brothers.

As the numbers joining Francis increased, so did the attention the group attracted. The attraction came not only from worried

families who were losing their sons, but also from the Benedictine monasteries and the wider church. Bishop Guido, who was becoming a friend and champion of Francis, advised the group to visit Rome and seek papal permission for their way of life. It was never Francis's intention to create a monastic 'order'; he only ever envisioned a small group of friends who would commit to serving

Saints

Jesus by caring for the poor and demonstrating the gospel through action as well as with words. But he was being forced to organize and legitimize his position and the trip to Rome necessitated the forming of a short 'rule'. This was a simple affair far from the lengthy Benedictine rule and was based on three verses from the Bible which had been key from the first days of the group who were later known as the 'Lesser Brothers' (Friars Minor).

The first verse, which was from Matthew 19:21, was 'Go, sell your possessions, and give to the poor, and you will have treasure in heaven; then come, follow me.' This called the group to absolute poverty. The brothers owned nothing except a simple peasant robe each. They wore them in all seasons and the robes would be lovingly patched over and over again. Francis's own robe is on display at the basilica in Assisi and one can see it has been repaired many times, it is a garment that was worn and worn, becoming an unusual patchwork of different dark brown fabrics.

The second called the brothers to trust God for all things: 'Take nothing for your journey, no staff, nor bag, nor bread, nor money – not even an extra tunic' (Luke 9:3). Christians are told to pray 'Give us today our daily bread', which really means 'Provide for me everything I need for this day.' Yet some of us continue to worry

about where 'this' will come from or how we will pay for 'that'. Circumstances often lead us to panic, but Jesus refuses to budge, 'Do not worry!' he tells us. God will provide, he can be trusted and will take care of us if only we would learn to allow him to do so.

The third and final rule was based on Luke 9:23: 'If any want to become my followers, let them deny themselves'. It carries with it a message of servanthood; to deny oneself means to promote others, preferring their needs over one's own. Much is often made of Francis's affinity with nature: he stopped to preach to the birds; he talked to the wolf who terrorized a village making it promise not to attack again and as he stretched out beneath the trees at La Verna birds came and covered his body. But Francis loved and cared for creation because  he loved first the creator. In his position as servant Francis took the example of Jesus 'Who, though he was in the form of God, did not count equality with God a thing to be grasped, but made himself nothing, taking the form of a servant...' (Philippians 2:6–7). He placed himself at the bottom of all the created things and from that lowly perspective he became able to value and love all creation. Possibly we have been so surprised by the attitude of Francis towards creation we have dismissed him as some sort of eco-warrior from the Middle Ages. In doing so we miss Francis's role as the servant to humanity. If we lose Francis in the treasured stories of preaching to creation we will fail to see him comforting the poor or bathing the wounds of the leper. For every animal story there are ten more about Francis caring for the poor.

One particularly tender story concerns a man with advanced leprosy. We can only imagine the extent to which the disease had ripped apart his body. Several of the friars had been tending to the patient but had been forced to stop; the man had become violent and, more concerning for the monks, was his screaming and blaspheming against the name of Jesus which was so precious to them. Francis stopped what he was doing when he heard the man's cries and the brother's complaints and knelt to serve the man himself. His new patient angrily demanded to be bathed. 'My sores smell so bad I cannot bear my own company,' he told Francis who prepared hot scented water and tenderly began to bathe the man from head to toe, all the time praying for him. As Francis bathed an oozing wound it miraculously dried with the skin knitting together as if it had never been touched by the disease. This continued and slowly as each part of the leper was washed the leprosy retreated. The man wept continually, not solely at the miraculous bodily healing he was receiving, but the inner process of reconciliation and redemption that was being worked in his heart. At last Francis was finished and the man could stand before him restored in body and reconciled to God.

To deny oneself by Luke 9:23 continues 'let them deny themselves and take up their cross daily and follow me'. Following St Francis's teaching we can start afresh each day to carry our cross and to put others first, assuming in ourselves a position of humility.

These three verses then were the summary of a very simple 'rule'. Francis was taking the monastic commitment to simplicity to its conclusion. Benedict had already forbidden monks personal possessions; Francis disallowed property and provisions of any kind, communal or otherwise. Another marked difference between the two orders was the friars' dedication to travelling and preaching, which seemed to contradict Benedict's vow of stability. Early on, Francis was pulled between a desire to spend his life in prayerful reflection – an ascetic life typical of the monastic tradition – and that of committing his life to action, spreading the gospel of Jesus through deeds as well as words. Francis was so torn he wrote to two of his most trusted friends for counsel. Sylvester the friar priest and Sister Clare both quickly replied that action through preaching was the way ahead for the brothers. Of course this was always coupled with prayer and it would be impossible to separate the two; however the advice was clear: the Order was to find its place amongst the people rather than as a cloistered community separated from the outside world.

Friars were sent out from their communities with some travelling locally from village to village, working in the fields side by side with the labourers and tending the sick at leper houses. Others took the gospel message further into France, Spain and Germany. Francis himself eventually travelled during the Fifth Crusade to Egypt. His personal mission was to convert the sultan al-Kamil to Christianity and in doing so put an end to the war. It was rather an idealistic expectation but nevertheless Francis travelled to meet him, sailing in cramped ships for weeks before reaching the blood bath that was Damietta. There were 100,000 men camped beside the River Nile in the sweltering August heat. Decomposing bodies floated on the river and the stench stuck in Francis's nose. Francis somehow convinced the rather disturbing figure of Cardinal Pelagius who was masterminding the Crusade to allow him to try to talk with the sultan. Pelagius had up till now refused all diplomatic solutions to end the war so it is surprising that Francis was allowed to go. It is possible that Pelagius expected to receive news of Francis's death before evening, for while the Saracens tolerated Christianity within their borders any attempt to openly convert a Muslim was punishable by death.

Francis spent two weeks in the Saracen camp and while he failed to convert the leader of the Muslim world he certainly left an impression on the sultan. Perhaps al-Kamil saw in Francis and his humble brothers a more Christ-like model of Christianity than he found on the battlefield or indeed saw in the pope and his

Clare of Assisi

No consideration of the place of Francis in history or his influence in the church today could be complete without his friend and sister in Christ: Clare (1194–1253). The love they had for each other was in no way physical, yet they loved and complemented each other as only the best examples of married couples can. Clare, in her cloister, was the contemplative Francis yearned to be, whereas he, walking the fields, was the active preacher she admired and would have loved to have become. Alas for Clare the only role for a woman in the church was to be hidden from the world and devoted to prayerful service of Christ in the abbey, and here the papal court sought to protect her even from the vow of poverty her and her sisters dedicated themselves to.

Clare was the daughter of a noble family of Assisi, a higher class and years younger than Francis. They met after he began to preach in the churches of the town. This was still in the early days of Francis's calling and he by no means had the ecclesiastical approval that followed

cardinals. After journeying to Jerusalem, enjoying the protection of the sultan as they travelled, Francis embarked on his long voyage home.

The Francis who appeared stumbling from the ship on its return to Italy some weeks/months later was a mere shadow of the man who left over a year before. Mentally his resolve had been shaken by the disappointment at not having been able to convert the sultan and physically he was much weaker. Malaria now coursed through his veins with regular debilitating ferocity. His eyes had suffered in the dry bright heat of the desert and he was going blind.

years later. He and Clare would meet, in the company of chaperones, to discuss the gospel and the example of Jesus. She became convinced that a life of poverty and service was her calling too and they began plotting an escape. The signal was to come from Bishop Guido during the Palm Sunday service when he gave her a palm leaf as a sign of his blessing. With the help of the brothers Clare made her escape to a nearby Benedictine monastery.

Many young women were to join Clare and quickly the Order of the Poor Ladies, which later became known as the Poor Clares, was established. Stories abound of her devotion to prayer and her heart for intercession as well as her own tales of service to the poor. It was Clare who, after the death of Francis, carried the ideal of the Franciscan life, fighting to keep his vision central to the order. For many years too Clare battled with Rome over the right to take a vow of poverty and just the day before her death the messenger finally arrived delivering into her hands the papal bull that affirmed her life's work.

Francis is said to have received stigmata – the wounds of Christ. *The Little Flowers of Saint Francis* (a contemporary biography or sayings of Francis and his brothers) tell of wounds in his hands and feet where black sores showed under the surface like the heads of nails. Other more recent writers suggest that the open sores were a sign he had contracted leprosy, the disease of the suffering people he constantly sought out. Whether these wounds were scars from the nails which hung Jesus from the cross or signs of the suffering leper is immaterial. In either case they were the wounds of Jesus and Francis was sharing in the sufferings of Christ.

The pain in Francis's eyes increased as the years passed. He was often forced to spend weeks in a darkened shelter. It was here in the midst of his deepest personal suffering that Francis composed his 'Canticle of the Sun' in which he praised God through the created elements, Brother Sun and Mother Earth. Francis was able to see the image of God in every created thing and would praise the creator in spite of the circumstances that might rob him of this duty and pleasure.

Jesus' call to Francesco Giovanni Bernadone was 'to rebuild my church' and this was the purpose that flowed from the man who became St Francis of Assisi. Everything he did and said was to bring glory and power to Jesus through his church. Whether that was by exploring and praising God through nature, interrupting parties to entertain locals and preach the gospel, caring for the sick or refusing all possession and instead relying solely on the provision of his Almighty God, Francis rebuilt the church wherever he walked. His life was short, dying in 1225 aged just forty-four, but the challenge he brought and continues to bring to the church echoes across the centuries.

Francis's 'Canticle of the Sun' is a prayer of praise and encourages one to stop and take notice. It urges people to look around and appreciate again – perhaps as they did first as children – the wonder of creation and through that deeper wonder of the Creator.

O most high, almighty, good Lord God,
To you belong praise, glory, honour and all blessing!
Praised be to my Lord God with all your creatures,
and especially our Brother Sun,
Who brings us the day and who brings us the light,

Fair is he and shines with a very great splendour:
O Lord, he signifies You to us!
Praised be my Lord for our Brother Wind,
And for air and cloud, calms and all weather
through which You uphold life in all creatures.
Praised be my Lord for our Sister Water,
who is very useful to us and humble and precious
and clean.
Praised be my Lord for our Brother Fire,
through whom You give us light in the darkness;
And he is bright and pleasant and very mighty and
strong.
Praised be my Lord for our Mother Earth,
Who does sustain us and keep us,
And who brings forth many fruits and flowers of
many colours, and grass.
Praised be my Lord for all those who pardon one
another for Your sake,
and endure weakness and tribulation,
Blessed are they who peaceably endure, for You,
O most high,
Shall give them a crown.
Praised be my Lord for our sister Death of the body,
from whom no one can escape.
Woe to those who die in mortal sin.
Blessed are they who are found walking by Your most
holy will, for the second death shall have no power
to do them harm.
Praise and bless the Lord, and give thanks to Him
and serve Him with great humility.

Bibliography

Adam, David, *Flame in My Heart: St Aidan for Today*, Triangle, 1997.

— —, *Tides and Seasons: Modern Prayers in the Celtic Tradition*, Triangle, 1989.

Barron, W. R. J. and Burgess, Glynn S. (eds.), *The Voyage of St Brendan: Representative Versions of the Legend in English Translation*, University of Exeter Press, 2002.

Bede, *Ecclesiastical History of the English People*, Price, Leo Shirley (trans.), and Farmer, D. H. (ed.), Penguin, 2003.

Brown, Michelle P., *How Christianity Came to Britain and Ireland*, Lion, 2006.

Butler, Alban, *Butler's Lives of the Saints*, Resources for Christian Living, 2000.

Celtic Daily Prayer: Inspirational Prayers and Readings from the Northumbria Community, Harper Collins, 2005.

Chesterton, G. K., *St Francis of Assisi*, Hodder and Stoughton, 1996.

The Cloud of Witnesses – A Companion to the Lesser Festivals and Holy Days of the Alternative Service Book, HarperCollins, 1980.

de Waal, Esther, *Seeking God: The Way of Saint Benedict*, Canterbury Press, 1999.

Dunn, Marilyn, *The Emergence of Monasticism*, Blackwell, 2003.

Mayer, Hans Eberhard, *The Crusades*, Oxford University Press, 1972.

Evans, G. R., *The History of Christian Europe*, Lion Hudson, 2008.

Farmer, David, *Oxford Dictionary of Saints*, Oxford University Press, 2004.

Foster, Richard J., *Streams of Living Water*, Harper, San Francisco, 2002.

Foxe, John, *Foxe's Book of Martyrs*, Berry, W. Grinton (ed.), Spire Publishing, 1973.

Hadjifoti, Litsa I., *Saint Paul: His Journeys Through Greece, Cyprus, Asia Minor and Rome*, Toubis 2006.

Kuzmanovski, Risto, *Ohrid and its Treasures*, Mikena–Bitola, 1994.

Lietzmann, Hans, *A History of the Early Church Volumes 1 to 4*, Meridian Books, 1961.

Mitton, Michael, *Restoring the Woven Cord*, Darton Longman and Todd, 1995.

Moss, Henry S., *The Birth of the Middle Ages 395–814*, Oxford University Press, 1969.

Okey, Thomas (trans.), *The Little Flowers of Saint Francis*, Dover Publications, 2003.

Simms, George Otto, *Brendan the Navigator: Exploring the Ancient World*, O'Brien Press, 2006.

Pernoud, Regine, *Martin of Tours: Soldier, Bishop, Saint*, Ignatius, 2006.

Sabatier, Paul, *The Road to Assisi: The Essential Biography of St Francis*,

Sweeney, Jon M. (ed.), Paraclete Press, 2005.
Sampson, Fay, *Visions and Voyages: The Story of Celtic Spirituality*, Lion, 2007.
Severin, Tim, *The Brendan Voyage,* Century Travellers, 1978.
Simpson, Ray, *Exploring Celtic Spirituality: Historic Roots for our Future*,
Hodder & Stoughton, 1995.
Spoto, Donald, *Reluctant Saint: The Life of Saint Francis*, Penguin
Compass, 2002.
The Story of Christian Spirituality, Lion Hudson, 2001.
Vardey, Lucinda, *Travelling with the Saints in Italy – Contemporary
Pilgrimages on Ancient Paths*, Paulist Press International, 2005.
Wakefield, Gavin, *Holy Places Holy People*, Lion Hudson, 2008.
Walker, Peter, *In the Steps of Saint Paul*, Lion Hudson, 2008.
White, Carolinne (trans., ed. and introduction), *Early Christian Lives,*
Penguin Classics, 2004.

Articles and Internet sites used for research

Christian Classics Etheral Library – various online writings including but not
limited to:
    de Voraigne, Jacobus, 'About The Golden Legend', vol. 6
    Schaff, Philip, 'History of the Christian Church: Mediaeval Christianity AD
    590–107' vol. IV'
    — —'History of the Christian Church: The Middle Ages AD 1049–1294 vol. V'
    — —'History of the Christian Church: The Middle Ages AD 1294–1517
    vol. VI'
    — —'The Apostolic Fathers with Justin Martyr and Irenaeus'
    'Abbot of Monte Cassino'
    'Benedict's Life and Rule'
    'Polycarp's Letter to the Philippians'
    'The Holy Rule of St Benedict by Saint Benedict'
    'The Life of Saint Polycarp'
    'The Martyrdom of Polycarp'

Christian History and Biography magazine – various past articles including but
not limited to:
    'Antony and the Desert Fathers: Christian History Interview: Discovering
    the Desert Paradox'
    'Antony and the Desert Fathers: Did You Know?'
    'Antony and the Desert Fathers: From the Editors – Models or Kooks?'
    'Spiritual Wisdom of the Desert Fathers'
    'The Blessing of Benedict'

Articles and Internet sites used for research (cont.)

http://198.62.75.1/www1/ofm/fra/FRAmain.html (Francsican experience)
www.christianity.net: 'Francis's Tenacious Lady'
www.churchtimeline.com (various articles)
www.coptic.net: *Encyclopedia Coptica*, including sayings of the Desert Fathers
www.newadvent.org: *Catholic Encyclopedia*
www.osb.org: 'The Order of Saint Benedict'
www.papalencyclicals.net: papal encyclicals including 'Slavorum Apostoli'
www.the-orb.net: 'Selections from Thomas of Celano: First and Second Lives of St Francis'